THE REALM OF FIG AND QUINCE

THE REALM OF FIG AND QUINCE

FROM MESOPOTAMIA TO THE MAGHREB

Ria Loohuizen

author of
The Elder
On Chestnuts

Translated from the Dutch
by
ALISSA VALLES

PROSPECT BOOKS
2010

First published in Great Britain in 2010 by Prospect Books, Allaleigh House, Blackawton, Totnes, Devon TQ9 7DL.

This book, entitled *Het rijk van kwee en vijg*, was first published in the Netherlands by Uitgeverij Atlas, Amsterdam in 2003.

BRITISH LIBRARY CATALOGUING IN PUBLICATION DATA:
A catalogue entry for this book is available from the British Library.

ISBN 978-1-903018-74-3
Typeset by Tom Jaine.
Printed in Great Britain at the Cromwell Press Group, Trowbridge.

Contents

Acknowledgements

I have listed in the bibliography the books I have consulted and in which I came across the quotations inserted in the text. Several have provided the ideas behind many of the recipes; I am very grateful for their pioneering work.

The photograph of the fig of page 75 is courtesy of Clare Pawley.

I am also thankful to my daughter, Alissa Valles, for the translation she made from the Dutch, as well as for her sound and humorous advice.

David Karp, quince expert and aficionado from Los Angeles, sent me very interesting information and articles, for which I am in his debt.

Cooking notes

When I mention olive oil in the recipes, I mean extra virgin oil (first cold pressing) for use unheated (in salads, etc.) and a lighter variety for frying; black pepper is always freshly ground, butter unsalted and parsley the flat-leaved kind.

Unless otherwise stated, the recipes are for 4 people.

Weights and measures

Oven temperatures

225°F	110°C	Gas ¼	Very cool
250°F	130°C	Gas ½	
275°F	140°C	Gas 1	Cool
300°F	150°C	Gas 2	
325°F	170°C	Gas 3	Moderate
350°F	180°C	Gas 4	
375°F	190°C	Gas 5	
400°F	200°C	Gas 6	Hot
425°F	220°C	Gas 7	
450°F	230°C	Gas 8	Very hot
475°F	240°C	Gas 9	

Measuring spoons and cups

½ teaspoon = 2.5 ml
1 teaspoon = 5 ml
1 tablespoon = 15 ml
¼ cup = 60 ml
⅓ cup = 80 ml
½ cup = 120 ml
1 cup = 240 ml

Jacopo Ligozzi (1547–1627), Fig and birds.

Introduction and itinerary

THE FIRST ORCHARD

And the Lord God planted a garden eastward in Eden; and there he put the man whom he had formed. And out of the ground made the Lord God to grow every tree that is pleasant to the sight and good for food; [...] And a river went out of Eden to water the garden; and from thence it was parted, and became into four heads. The name of the first is Pison: that is it which compasseth the whole land of Havilah, where there is gold; [...] And the name of the second river is Gihon: the same is it that compasseth the whole land of Ethiopia. And the name of the third river is Hiddekel: that is it which goeth toward the east of Assyria. And the fourth river is Euphrates.

Genesis 2:8–14

To begin at the beginning, we begin at the Beginning: Genesis. Where on the newly created earth did the Great Gardener plant his Garden of Eden, between those four named rivers? The indications are vague: 'eastward'. When we think of the Middle East, the Holy Land, what suggests itself is the image of a desert: yellow and arid, not green and fertile. One exception to this is the fertile plain of Mesopotamia (the name means literally 'between two rivers').

The majority of historians accept that the First Orchard was located in the area between the Euphrates and Tigris rivers in ancient Mesopotamia or what is now Iraq. It is an area that stretches northwards from the Persian Gulf to the mountains of Armenia and to the east from the Syrian desert to the Zagros mountains. Crucially, it contains a fertile alluvial plain, irrigated in antiquity by a network of canals. The southern part of this area has long been considered the cradle of civilization, even if today it may be difficult to identify Iraq with Paradise.

If the Tigris and Euphrates are two of the rivers of Eden, then the Gihon named in Genesis may possibly be the Nile, described as encompassing 'the whole land of Ethiopia'. The first, Pison, has never been identified.

Bible scholars and theologians of all denominations love to get their teeth into questions such as the first rivers of the Creation and their debates sometimes yield interesting theories. One of them is worth mentioning, if only because it sets the world on its head.

Mormons regard the 'Book of Moses', discovered in the early 1800s by the famous Egyptologist Champollion in what was believed to be a royal casket and bought for $6,000 by a woman who belonged to the Church of Jesus Christ of Latter Day Saints, as part of holy scripture. The Mormon interpretation of this book, and of Genesis, is that four rivers flowed together, making one. And where in the world do we find four rivers flowing together? The Mormons believed the confluence of the Mississippi, Missouri, Ohio and Illinois rivers is the only geographical location that conforms to the description in Genesis.

This book's journey will trace the arc made by both fig and quince from their paradisal origins to the markets and tables of today. These fruits travelled with the Medes and Persians of ancient times, and then with the Phoenicians, Greeks and Romans; a voyage that led through Turkey, Greece, Italy, France, Spain and North Africa. As we follow them in search of the most delicious recipes, we are accompanied by poets and prose writers, cartographers and artists. What better point of departure than the Garden of Eden?

THE FIRST BITE

> *When Eve knew* in her mind *that she was naked*
> *She quickly sewed fig-leaves, and sewed the same for the*
> *man.*
> *She'd been naked all her days before,*
> *But till then, till that apple of knowledge, she hadn't had*
> *the fact on her mind.*
>
> D.H. Lawrence,
'Figs' from *Birds, Beasts and Flowers*, 1923

The history of food has an ominous beginning: someone bites into an apple and look at the consequences! After that first bite, we are told, 'the eyes of them both were opened, and they knew that they were naked'. How do they respond? 'They sewed fig leaves together, and made themselves aprons' (Genesis 3:7–8).

This would make the fig leaf the first item of clothing in human history. One leaf was evidently not enough to make an 'apron', although the figures in most sculptures and paintings have to do with just one. The Bible contains many other references to and parables about the fig; fig trees were common in Palestine. The passage 'every man dwelt safely under his vine and under his fig tree' evokes a time of happiness, prosperity, safety and security: the ultimate life of peace and well-being.

> *Then, Thyrsus, you must stop your mouth with sweetness,*
> *Eat only honeycomb and the best figs.*
>
> Theocritus, *Idylls*
> (3rd century BC, trans. Robert Wells)

In some traditions, the fig is more closely woven into the fabric of Eden than mere modest cover-all. These claim the fruit plucked by Eve was the fig, not the apple. The

Creation mosaics in St Mark's in Venice depict just this interpretation of the myth.

It was in Andalusia, southern Spain, that I first saw a real-life fig tree and ate a fresh fig, so different from the dried version. The great expectations I had, freed at last from the flavourless, shapeless and colourless food of my youth, were crushed. I had an 'Is that all?' feeling similar to when I first confronted an artichoke and, after a lot of leaf-pulling and choking I was left with a great pile of debris and a tiny mouthful of flesh.

A few years later, when I went to live in California, a veritable cornucopia, my culinary awareness developed with alarming speed and for months I ate something new, something I had never eaten before, every week. At the end of my decade on that coast there were still some products I hadn't tasted. In these times of winter strawberries and summer cabbages this may be hard to imagine, but until the early seventies, I did not know zucchini, or pumpkin, parsnip, papaya, broccoli or even bell peppers – let alone the dozens of varieties of fresh greens and root vegetables that were on offer there.

There was a fig tree in my garden and by that time I learned to appreciate what Elizabeth David calls 'one of the exquisite pleasures of the Mediterranean': picking a fig, warmed by the sun, straight from the tree, splitting it open and devouring it on the spot. And I learned to deal with the abundant summer harvest by making jams, tarts and preserves. This period has left me with a soft spot for one of the softest, most delicate of fruits, which in its dried state can be tough as leather – one of the enduring contradictions in nature.

THE GOLDEN APPLE

> *Offering*
> *A yellow-coated pomegranate, figs like lizards' necks*
> *A handful of half-rosy part-ripe grapes,*
> *A quince all delicate-downed and fragrant-fleeced,*
> *A walnut winking out from its green shell,*
> *A cucumber with the bloom on it from its leaf-bed,*
> *And a ripe gold-coated olive – dedicated*
> *To Priapus friend of travellers, by Lamon the gardener,*
> *Begging strength for his limbs and his trees.*
> Philippos (1st century AD; trans. Edwin Morgan)

Like the fig, the quince boasts a long history; in literary terms an even longer one than the fig. It plays an important role in Greek myth and is by many assumed to be the 'golden apple of the Hesperides', which Hercules seeks in one of his labours.

For years I had admired these old fruits, covered with their strange down, in the still-lifes painted in the seventeenth century, and in the markets of France and Spain. When I started to cook with them, it was magic to see those hard yellow astringent things turn into the colour of the most exquisite orange gem. *Membrillo*, quince paste or quince cheese, was an ubiquitous item in Spain, where it was served with a piece of old Manchego cheese, a classic combination. When I returned to the Netherlands the first 'guest workers' were arriving from Spain, Turkey and Morocco, and from their surprising cuisine I learned how to combine fruit and meat, for which the quince, retaining its shape and gaining in flavour in cooking, is so eminently suitable.

Giovanna Garzoni (1600–1670).

The historical fig

The fig is a mysterious fruit with many special properties and huge sex appeal. The fruit is often compared to the female genitalia, but at the same time is associated with the male sex.

> *Every fruit has its secret.*
>
> *The fig is a very secretive fruit.*
> *As you see it standing growing, you feel at once it is symbolic:*
> *And it seems male.*
> *But when you come to know it better, you agree with the Romans, it is female.*
>
> D.H. Lawrence,
> 'Figs' from *Birds, Beasts and Flowers*, 1923

For the Hellenes it was the sacred fruit of the lustful and ever-thirsty god Dionysus. If the fruit seems to mimic the female pudenda, the tree is often thought to represent the male. Dionysus placed a phallus made of fig wood on the grave of Polyhymnos instead of carrying out a promised favour, and still today a phallus cut from fig wood is carried aloft on the festivals and feast days of Bacchus. And to think that the fig leaf is at the same time a symbol of modesty.

An altar from Ostia showing the discovery of Romulus and Remus, now preserved at the Palazzo Massimo in Rome. Garlands of figs are seen hanging to each side.

It was this customary symbolism that prompted Horace to write in his first *Satire*, 'I was once the trunk of a wild fig, a useless log [fig wood never had much of a reputation]: when the carpenter, in doubt whether he should make a stool or a Priapus [i.e. phallus] of me, determined that I should be a god.'

Roman mythology has it that Romulus and Remus were suckled by the she-wolf under the fig tree, the roots of which had stayed their basket when adrift on the Tiber.

In other contexts, the fig signifies fertility, prosperity and well-being: some say that if you dream of a fig tree, it is a prophecy of riches, good fortune and a happy old age. The fig is a traditional part of Pesach, Jewish Easter, which explains the saying 'like figs after Easter' or something that comes too late. The greening of the tree was thought by the Greeks to herald the coming of spring: 'When a man sees leaves on a fig-tree as large as the mark that a crow makes, then is the spring sailing time,' wrote Hesiod.

The symbolic sexual potence of the fruit was embodied in the universal Mediterranean gesture of 'the

John Leech's more humorous depiction of the discovery of Rome's founders.

fist' or *fico*. Partridge explains in his *Dictionary of Slang*: 'A contemptuous gesture made by thrusting the thumb forth between the first two fingers.' Contemptuous it might have been, but it was also an amulet – to ward off evil spirits – or an invitation to dalliance: you guessed which by the demeanour of the fist-maker. Calumny and insult was the general idea in early-modern Europe, however, as Pistol thought in Henry V: 'A *fico* for thy friendship!' The English often called the gesture 'the Spanish fig' (we have a tendency to ascribe to foreigners much unpleasantness). Here too is the origin of the expression, 'I don't give a fig'. Some modest lexicographers suggest this refers to the cheapness of dried figs, but more likely we are dealing with something more earthy.

It is very probable that the fig tree originated in the fertile area in the south of ancient Arabia. It is certain that both the Sumerians (2900 BC) and the Assyrians (2000 BC) knew it. The fig was cultivated for centuries and gradually reached Syria, Turkey and the Mediterranean, helped along by the industriousness and colonial drive of sea-faring peoples. By around 1600 BC it could be found on Crete. The Phoenicians and Greeks were responsible for spreading fig cultivation throughout the ancient world. The Phoenicians colonized the islands of Cyprus, Rhodes, Sicily, Malta and Corsica, followed by the coastal regions of North Africa. Archaeological research has established that this ancient trading people planted figs more in their colonies than in their homelands.

For the ancient Greeks, figs were an auspicious and luxurious article; they were presented as medals or strung into wreaths for Olympic athletes. Fig trees were sacred, and it was forbidden to export them, and those who did so were reported to the authorities by so-called sycophants. Among the first figs in literature are those mentioned – three times – in Homer's *Odyssey*, thought to have been composed in approximately the ninth century BC. From Greece, fig cultivation spread along the northern coast of the Mediterranean and the Adriatic to Italy, where the fig tree features in the myth of Rome's founding.

Seventeen hundred years after Phoenician colonization, the same trading routes were travelled by the Moors, who introduced the fig to Spain, Portugal and France from North Africa. The Arabs loved figs more than any other fruit.

> *I use 'sycophant' in its original sense, as a wretch who flatters the prevailing party by informing against his neighbours, under pretence that they are exporters of prohibited figs.*
> Samuel Coleridge (1772–1834) *Biographia Literaria*

The botanical fig

*F*icus carica is a member of the family *Moraceae*, which also includes the mulberry and the breadfruit, and various tropical *ficus* varieties which produce edible fruit for consumption by local human and animal populations. Other varieties, which do not bear fruit, are *Ficus elastica* (rubber plant) and *Ficus benjamina*, both well-known pot plants.

The fig tree – with the olive tree the ultimate symbol of the Mediterranean – is a tree with crooked branches and a ragged way of growing, a pale grey bark and a unique shape, which can't be confused with any other tree; it reaches a height of 5.5 metres. The alternate leaves are thick and leathery, hand-shaped, with three to five lobes; they grow to between ten and twenty centimetres in length. The fig tree flourishes in a warm, dry climate and although it doesn't enjoy a heavy frost, some varieties do well in northern Europe, where it rarely bears sweet fruit. In humid climates the fig tree is susceptible to diseases like rust and the fruit can be spoiled by fermentation caused by insects.

The blossoms are held in a kind of sack (the syconium). These flowers then develop into thousands of tiny fruits, also held within the syconium – each of which contains about 1,500. Each fig looks like an inside-out strawberry –

From The Encyclopaedia Britannica, *11th edition.*

full of what look like seeds but are actually little fruits.

> *There was a flower that flowered inward, womb-ward;*
> *Now there is a fruit like a ripe womb.*
> *It was always a secret.*
> *That's how it should be, the female should always be*
> *secret.*

D.H. Lawrence,
'Figs' from *Birds, Beasts and Flowers*, 1923

The whole process of fruition is complicated and for many species of fig depends on a gnat-sized insect, the fig-wasp, which pollinates the flower in its attempt to reproduce itself. Unfortunately for the wasp, this process usually leads to more figs than wasps. Even in the fourth century BC Aristotle knew that the wild fig depended on that little wasp's input and wrote a treatise on it. During the Roman empire, new kinds of fig appeared which were able to self-pollinate and did not rely on the fig-wasp. The most important self-pollinating variety is called the 'common fig' and produces two crops a year. The success of these varieties allowed the fig to greatly increase its range, outside the narrow band of climates which suited the wasp. The botanical details of the fig tree are too extensive and complex to spell out in this book. They may easily be found by the interested reader; a good starting-point is the entry 'Fig' in Alan Davidson's indispensable work *The Oxford Companion to Food*.

The fig's sugar content of over 55 per cent makes it one of the sweetest fruits. The fig's peel is thin, edible and feels like a piece of chamois cloth.

Dried figs come in the most varied forms – large and small, in baskets, boxes and strung together – and are available all year round. For the 'dried harvest' the fruits are left to dry on the trees and then gathered mechanically when they fall, at intervals of two or three weeks. They go on drying in the sun until their water content has shrunk to less than 17 per cent.

In northern Europe fresh figs appear on the market in August or September and are usually available until March. The great majority are black or blue Turkish figs, but the green-skinned fig is also imported from Italy and Brazil, among other places. Because it is such a delicate fruit it can be difficult to find unblemished, yet reasonably ripe figs, but it is always worth a search. Slightly unripe, half-green, half-purple figs will go on ripening if left out of the fridge.

The proper way to eat a fig, in society,
Is to split it in four, holding it by the stump,
And open it, so that it is a glittering, rosy, moist,
Honied, heavy-petalled four petalled flower.

D.H. Lawrence,
'Figs' from *Birds, Beasts and Flowers*, 1923

The medicinal fig

Figs are fitter for medicine than any other profit that is gotten by the fruit of them.

Nicholas Culpeper, *The Complete Herbal*

Figs contain more raw fibre – both digestible and indigestible – than any other fruit or vegetable. They have a mild laxative effect.

According to Culpeper, 'a syrup made of the leaves or green fruits is excellent for coughs, hoarseness and shortness of breath and all diseases of the chest and lungs. It is also very good for dropsy and falling-sickness' (*The Complete Herbal*, 1649).

The milky juice or latex in the fruit stems helps against warts. However, it can cause a rash with those who have very sensitive skin. The fig contains a natural substance, psoralens, that has been used for thousands of years for pigmentation problems. Psoralens also aids tanning of the skin.

The Roman writer and naturalist Pliny the Elder (AD 23/24–79) wrote of the fruit in his *Natural History*: 'Figs have a restorative effect. They increase the strength of the young and maintain the health and appearance of the old, making them look younger and less wrinkled.'

NUTRITIONAL VALUE OF DRIED FIGS (PER 100 GRAMS)

Calories 274
Water 23%
Protein 4.3%
Fat 1.3%
Carbohydrates 69%
Fibre 5.8%

Percentage of recommended daily allowance
  Vitamin A 1.6
  Thiamin B1 7.1
  Riboflavin B2 6.2
  Niacin 3.9
  Vitamin C -
  Calcium 15.8
  Phosphorus 9.6
  Iron 30
  Sodium 0.8
  Potassium 4

Fresh figs are a rich source of natural fruit sugar and iron and are about 50 calories a piece.

The historical quince

A quince preserved through the winter, given to a lady.

I'm a quince, saved over from last year, still fresh,
My skin young, not spotted or wrinkled, downy as
The new-born,
As though I were still among my leaves. Seldom
Does winter yield such gifts, but for you, my queen,
Even the snows and frosts bear harvests like this.
Antiphilos (1st century AD; translated W.S. Merwin)

The quince, which originates in Persia and Anatolia, can boast an ancient ancestry. It owes its old names, *Melon kydonion* (Kydonian apple), *Pyrus cydonia*, *Cydonia oblonga*, to the Cretan city of Kythonia, now Chaniá, where the best and most fragrant quinces were said to grow. The fruit was known in Greece in the ninth century BC and from there it travelled to Italy, Spain and beyond. The first reports of quince imported to northern Europe occur in English documents dating from 1275. In the sixteenth and seventeenth centuries it was cultivated in England and used both in cooking and medicine. With the arrival of soft fruit – fruit that could be eaten without being cooked – the quince rapidly decreased in popularity.

'Golden apples', thought to have been quinces, play an important role in Greek mythology as the playthings of gods and demi-gods, and as the fruit of destiny, as in the myth of Atalanta and Hippomenes. Any suitor of the legendary beauty Atalanta had to beat her in a race in order to win her hand, which was unfortunate for them as she was the swiftest mortal alive, and anyone who lost against her would die. Hippomenes, though, was clever enough to take advice from Aphrodite, who told him to drop three golden apples during the race. Atalanta stooped to pick up each apple in turn and narrowly lost to Hippomenes. On old Greek murals and vase paintings we find bears holding quinces, an allusion to Atalanta, who was suckled by a bear. Heracles also encountered the golden apple. His eleventh labour was to pick them from the garden of the Hesperides, from the tree which Mother Earth (Gaia) had given as a wedding gift to Hera. This tree was guarded by Atlas. Heracles offered to carry Atlas' globe while Atlas fetched the golden apples for him. But when Atlas came back with the apples, he found the freedom from his erstwhile burden so delicious that he tried to trick Heracles into holding the globe for ever.

In another famous myth Hera, Aphrodite and Athena joined in a contest for the golden apple, thrown among the guests at a wedding of the gods by Eris, the goddess of discord, who was angry at being excluded from the party. The golden apple had an inscription carved upon it: 'For the fairest one.' Zeus decided that the shepherd Paris would have the task of choosing between the three fair goddesses. Each of them offered Paris a bribe for the apple, Aphrodite saying that she would give him the most beautiful woman in the world – Helen of Troy – as his wife. Paris chose Aphrodite, which decision led in the end to the Trojan War.

Despite this, the apple of Aphrodite, or Venus, became a symbol of love and fertility. Plutarch reported that a Greek bride would nibble a quince before entering the bridal chamber, 'in order that the first greeting may not be disagreeable or unpleasant' (*Roman Questions*, 3.65). In some parts of Greece the tradition of offering a quince to a couple of newlyweds still exists. In an English family album of 1725 we find a groom's grandfather offering a basket of quinces to wish the couple happiness. It was said that a married couple would not be happy until they had eaten quinces together.

The botanical quince

Cydonia oblonga; Fam: *Rosaceae*.

> *Apart from its fruit, the beauty of an old quince tree makes it worth a place in my garden, with its sweeping pendulous branches, knotted and gnarled grotesquely, distinct in their dark colour, and quite unlike the ordinary fruit tree in effect. The large cup-shaped flowers of white or flesh pink are beautiful, hanging like single roses from the tips of every side shoot among the soft rounded leaves, silvery white beneath. And when in autumn the boughs hang yet lower beneath their load of fruits, whose colour outvies the golden leaves, few trees grown for effect are finer than this 'golden apple of the Hesperides'.*
>
> William Robinson, *Flora and Sylva*, 1904

The quince still grows in the wild in the regions in which it originated: Iran and Anatolia, Asia Minor, the Caucasus, Armenia, Georgia and Saudi Arabia. It has been cultivated for millennia, beginning in the irrigated orchards of ancient Mesopotamia.

Today the quince is grown in the countries surrounding the Mediterranean Sea – Turkey above all – and in Latin America, for instance Argentina which produces 20,000 tonnes annually.

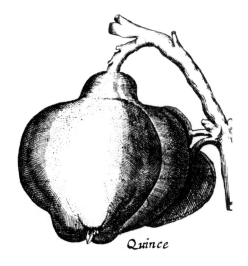

Quince

From A Book of Fruits and Flowers, *1653.*

The quince tree is a small tree that can reach a height of four to six metres, while its knarled branches reach a bent, shrub-like breadth of three to four and a half metres. Young twigs are covered with a pale, greyish wool. The leaves are ovate or elliptical, five to ten centimetres in length and four to six centimetres wide, dark green on top and pale underneath, with a thick, felt-like layer (particularly in the early stages of growth). In autumn the leaves turn yellow. The solitary blossoms at the tips of the short twigs are about five centimetres across, pink or white, and bloom towards the end of May and the beginning of June, after all leaves have sprouted. The late bloom has the advantage that the quince tree is hardly ever affected by frost in colder climates. The tree is self-pollinating and fertilized by bees.

The quince is barely susceptible to parasites and disease. Fruit can be kept for three or four months after harvesting, as long as they are stored separately in a cool, airy place. Dried, preserved, or blanched and frozen they can be kept for months.

The quince turns from green to a lovely golden yellow and its shape is that of a bumpy pear, apple or cross between the two, with a strong fragrance. Some types have a layer of grey down which can easily be rubbed off. The flesh is firm, aromatic and coarse-grained around the core. Cut open, the flesh quickly turns brown, the reason why it must be put in water with lemon juice or cooked immediately. One fruit can weigh up to a pound. The harvest is in October and November. Each fruit contains five packets of eight to sixteen brown seeds, stuck together in a slightly flattened egg shape, which become slimy when moist. The pips contain prussic acid, which is harmless as it is not released during the preparation of the fruit.

Quince trees flourish in cool as well as warm regions, but the fruit only becomes large and soft in a southern climate.

Other related varieties, like the Japanese quince (*Chanomeles japonica*), a low creeping shrub with magnificent red blossoms and small yellow apples, are often used as ornamental plants in parks and streets. The fruit of this plant is also edible.

The medicinal quince

*The expressed juice, taken in small quantities, is a mild,
astringent stomachic medicine, of efficacy in sickness,
vomiting, eructations and purgings.*
Nicholas Culpeper, *The Complete Herbal*

The first report of the healing effect of the quince
dates back to the fifth century BC and comes from
Hippocrates, the 'father of medicine', who recommends
it in cases of fever and diarrhoea. Dioscorides, author of
De Materia Medica, a treatise on more than five hundred
herbs and plants and their medical uses, describes
various quince remedies. One remedy involving raw,
boiled or honey-preserved quince, as well as a quince
wine, is recommended to counteract haemorrhages, as in
excessive menstruation, and quince is also used against
cholera. Pliny the Elder, too, recognized the beneficial
effects of quince, noting down twenty-one applications
in his *Natural History*, including the use of quince against
baldness, and he claimed: 'The down on the skin of
quinces heals furuncles.'

The gifted medieval nun and mystic Hildegard of
Bingen found the quince useful in the treatment of gout
and rheumatic conditions. Other famous medical men
such as the Fleming Rembert Dodoens (Dodonaeus) and

the Englishman Nicholas Culpeper, also used the fruit and its derivatives. On voyages of discovery during the fifteenth and sixteenth centuries, quinces preserved in honey or wine were a proven remedy for scurvy.

In the nineteenth century, wine made from quinces was popular in treatments to relieve asthma. An elixir was also made from the raw juice mixed with lemon juice to treat sore throats, diarrhoea and intestinal bleeding. It was once used to fortify singers' voices. In Germany an elixir of this kind is still on the market. The remedy counteracts infections of the stomach and mucous membranes and it is also used in cosmetics.

In Chinese medicine, the bark of the tree is used as an astringent in case of ulcers and the flesh is used as an antidote to poison, as a remedy for flatulence and as a digestive.

Quince pips contain a gummy substance of which an eye lotion is made, as well as a jelly used against sore throats. This natural gel was called *Mucilago seminum cydoniae* (quince pip slime) in old pharmacopaeias. Culpeper prescribed it for 'curing painful breasts in women'.

Do not discard the pips when you make a dish for which the core has to be removed: dry them and save them for using as a pectin for jams and jellies.

Quince leaves contain 11 per cent tannin and as such are suitable to be used in the tanning of leather.

NUTRITIONAL VALUE OF QUINCE (PER 100 GRAMS OF FRUIT)

Calories 57
Water 84%
Protein 0.4%
Fat 0.1%
Carbohydrates 15%

Percentage of recommended daily allowance
Vitamin A 0.8
Thiamin B1 1.4
Riboflavin B2 5.0
Niacin 1.1
Vitamin C 33
Calcium 1.4
Phosphorus 2.1
Iron 7.0
Sodium -
Potassium 4.2

A short history of sugar

Because so many recipes – candy, preserves, jams and jellies and desserts – in this book involve sugar, it seems appropriate to say something in depth about the origins of sugar, one of those daily articles of consumption that are so ordinary we never stop to think that they were once 'invented'.

SUGAR CANE

It was the Arabs who discovered something that completely transformed the taste of food: sugar. From Persia and Egypt the cultivation of sugar spread westward by way of islands such as Cyprus and Rhodes and further along the coast of the Mediterranean. The word derives from the Arabic word *zoukkar* (Sanskrit *zarkara*, Greek *sakkharon* and Latin *saccharin*). Sugar cane (*Saccharum officinarum*), a plant from the family of grasses (*Gramineae*), was at first only chewed for the enjoyment of its sweet taste; Arab alchemists then crystallized and refined sugar by pressing the stalks and eliminating non-saccharine elements by means of condensation on a wood fire. Thus a brown pulp was formed, which turned into crystals after cooling off. This pulp was called *khurat al milh*, from which the word 'caramel' was derived. They continued to improve the process of refining, purifying with milk and pouring the pulp into conical moulds. This produced *tabarseth* or sugar loaves, from which people chipped off pieces for use. In Europe the first sugar cane plantations were established in the twelfth century in Sicily and Andalusia by the Moors, and by the fifteenth century by Spanish and Portuguese explorers in both the Old and New World. During the Renaissance the Venetian spice traders imported sugar from the East Indies.

Although the earliest use in the Near and Middle East was for preserving and candying fruit, in the Middle Ages monks in Europe began to candy the stalks and other parts of herb plants (like Angelica) and the peel of citrus fruits.

MEDICINE

Initially sugar was a luxury item, available only as an expensive medicine. It was used as a sneezing powder and because it stops fermentation, it was also known as an antiseptic. Sugar was also important for its preservative effect, of course, particularly in the tropical countries in which it originated.

Up to the beginning of the nineteenth century, European countries tried to satisfy their demand for sugar by imports from their own colonies. They imported the rough pulp to be refined in the mother country; in this way, sugar refineries were established in many port cities in Europe. As sugar cultivation increased, sugar prices went down, and sugar ceased to be a luxury article.

Nowadays, the manufacture of cane sugar yields as its by-products syrup, rum, alcohol, fuel, cattle feed, while the pressed stalks are used to make paper.

SUGAR BEET

In 1747 a Berlin chemist named Marggraf discovered that beet juice contains sugar. He was under the impression, however, that the amount in the plant (*Beta vulgaris*) was not sufficient to warrant the development of an extraction method. About forty years later Achard, one of his former students, looked at the experiments again and in 1802 his successful attempt – supported by the Prussian king Frederick-William III – resulted in the first sugar factory in Germany. The technique of fabricating sugar was perfected and beets with an increasing sugar level (up to 20 per cent) were cultivated. In Napoleonic France, too, where the Revolution and ensuing international conflicts paralysed the cane sugar trade, the procedure was adopted and a small sugar industry emerged.

Unlike the process of pressing rough pulp from sugar cane, the process of making sugar from beets is accompanied by an unpleasant sickly odour, as anyone knows who has lived near a sugar factory.

Sugar, above all white refined sugar, has acquired a bad reputation over the past century, because it has been said to cause obesity and hyperactivity (ADHD) and as a side effect increases the chances of cardio-vascular diseases.

However, we should be aware that this is not the fault of sugar, which itself contains no harmful substances, but of its excessive consumption, which results in an unbalanced diet. Sugar provides fast energy but contains no other nutritional value or vitamins. One consequence of the changing image of sugar is the appearance on the market of many alternatives to white sugar.

The forms of sugar now generally available are granulated sugar, soft brown sugar (moscovado, light or dark), powdered sugar, sugar cubes (white or brown), cane sugar (usually pricier than beet sugar), and candy sugar (white or brown 'rocks'). The word candy derives from the Persian word *qand* and from *khanda*, as it was called in Sanskrit.

I use cane sugar to make vanilla sugar, by putting a few vanilla pods with the sugar in a well-sealed jar or bottle which I top up regularly. This is much fuller-flavoured than shop-bought packets, which usually depend on vanilla extract. Vanilla pods can be re-used, even when they have been cooked in a compote or syrup. Just rinse them off and put them in the sugar pot once dry. I use this sugar as a dusting for quince paste.

Preserving sugar is granulated sugar with the addition of gelatine, citric acid, preservatives and vegetable oil – to make jam or jelly using less sugar per unit of weight. Nowadays there are also organic versions of cane sugar and granulated beet sugar, made from plants that have not been sprayed with pesticides.

People who cannot or do not wish to eat sugar can use honey in many cases, or make the old Roman sweeteners *passum* or *defrutum*.

PASSUM

Soak 100 grams raisins in half a litre of red wine for two to three days. Purée the mixture and put it through a fine strainer; it is now ready for use. For an extra sweet version, use a sweet red wine.

DEFRUTUM

Boil 1 litre of grape juice (from red or black grapes) until one third remains. Bottle and use as desired.

Membrillo, theme and variations

What His Lordship the Governor should eat now in my opinion in order to remain healthy and strong, is a hundred or so wafers and a few thin slices of membrillo, which calm the stomach and stimulate the appetite.

Cervantes, *Don Quixote*

A lmost all the countries we will visit on our journey have in common one or other form of quince paste, of which the best known is the Spanish *carne de membrillo* or *dulce de membrillo*: in its purest form a purée of fresh quinces cooked with their equal weight in sugar until almost all the moisture has evaporated. It is a good way to preserve quinces to eat all year round. Before sugar was invented this was done with *passum* or *defrutum*, or with honey: the ancient Romans called the fruit *melimelum*, honey-apple, a reference to the way they preserved the fruit. The great Roman doctor Galen talks of this very conserve: 'In Syria is made a quince-cake which lasts for such a long time that containers packed with it are exported to Rome. It is made from honey and the flesh of quinces that has been pulped and boiled with honey.'

Whether it is called *quittenkäse, quince cheese, kytonopasto, cotignac, coudougnat, codogniato, cotognata, bimbriyo, membrillo, kweekoeckjes* or *ladrilhos de marmelo*, and whether it is poured in the form of a thin layer, or an animal, or cut into cubes and squares, the result is a sweet of a gorgeous orange-pink colour, with a subtle aroma and flavour, which can be enjoyed on its own, with coffee or with a piece of mature cheese – the classic Spanish combination *membrillo con Manchego* indicates that a goat's milk or sheep's milk cheese is traditionally preferred.

In the course of centuries, various countries introduced changes, adding spices, herbs, rose or orange blossom water, wine and nuts. Nostradamus, born in the south of France and better known for his prophetic rather than for his culinary gifts, offers different ways to prepare *pâtes de coing* and always kept them in *boîtes de sapin*, boxes made of split wood. Depicted in so many still-lifes of the sixteenth and seventeenth centuries, *cotignac* has been made in Orléans since the fifteenth century: Joan of Arc was offered some after the siege of Orléans in 1429.

 BASIC RECIPE FOR MEMBRILLO

> **Warning:** *boiling down the quince cheese is accompanied by a great deal of sputtering from the dangerously hot mixture: use a ladle with a long handle and protect your arm and hand with a sleeve or oven glove.*

Choose good unblemished quinces, the yellower, the better. Wash or rub the down off and put the whole fruits in a pan, just covered by water. Bring to the boil and let cook till done on medium high heat. Depending on the size and variety of fruit, this can take 20 minutes to one hour. Quinces are cooked when you can easily pierce them with a fork; by then the skin has usually burst. Take the quinces from the cooking liquid with a slotted spoon, put them on a plate and let them cool, covered with paper towels or a tea towel.

Remember that the water left over after boiling quinces is often so fragrant that you can use it to make quince jelly, especially if you reduce it first with the peel and cores you have removed from the cooked quinces.

Peel the quinces and remove the core. Purée the flesh with a blender or a handheld mixer.

Weigh the pulp and put it in a pan with a heavy bottom with an equal weight of sugar (ordinary granulated sugar). I always use an enamelled cast-iron Le Creuset pan. Using something with a heavy bottom prevents the pulp from sticking or caramelizing.

Bring the mixture to a boil and let it thicken, stirring all the while, until it almost forms a ball. This can take half an hour or longer, while the mixture stops simmering and begins to sigh softly, creating little craters. It is ready when a mark made in the fondant-like mixture does not close up anymore. Be patient and don't stop stirring too soon, or the paste will not become firm enough!

Pour or spoon the thickened mixture into an oven tray or a shallow dish in which you have sprinkled some caster sugar (flavoured with vanilla). Make an even layer 1 to 2 centimetres thick. Let it cool completely. You can also let the quince cheese set in smaller earthenware dishes.

When the quince cheese has cooled you know right away whether it has worked: when you cut into it, it should not stick – or barely stick – to the knife. If it seems too soft, you would do best to return it to the pan and let it boil down some more. Cut the paste into cubes, sprinkle them with some more sugar and let them dry overnight. Some suggest putting the cubes or paste to dry in a very low oven. If the mixture has been properly boiled down, however, this is not necessary.

Store the quince candy in split-wood boxes with bay leaves in between the cubes. They can be kept for several years in a dry, airy place – but who could resist them for that long?

🐌 VARIATIONS

For a more Middle Eastern flavour, prepare the basic recipe up to setting-point. Remove the pan from the heat and stir a teaspoon (or more, according to taste and quantity of paste) of ground cardamom and some whole pine nuts into the mixture.

In her unequalled *Book of Jewish Food*, Claudia Roden gives a Sephardic version which adds the juice of half a lemon to each 2 kg of quince. Sometimes cloves are added as well.

Nostradamus, or Michel de Nostradamus (1503–1566), in his version of the Provençal *coudougnat,* adds wine, which gives the paste a slightly sharp alcoholic flavour, which contrasts well with the flowery, sweet honey. Use a cheap, light and fluid honey, as it serves only as a sweetener and should not overpower the quince. This recipe calls for typically excessive medieval quantities, but you can always give it away at Christmas.

❧ NOSTRODAMUS' COUDOUGNAT

> *2 kg ripe quinces*
> *1 litre red wine*
> *approx. 1 ½ kg honey (300 g honey to 500 g fruit)*
> *1 ½ tsp ground cinnamon*
> *1 ½ tsp ground ginger*
> *½ tsp ground cloves*

Peel the quinces, remove the cores and put aside both peel and cores. Put the quinces in a pan and add wine until the fruit is just covered. Cook the quinces on a low flame.

Strain the quinces, purée them and weigh the pulp.

Put the pulp in a thick-bottomed pan and add honey (300 g to 500 g fruit pulp). Add the spices and mix well.

Boil down the purée and pour it out as described in the basic recipe for *membrillo.*

In the time of Nostradamus this was cut into squares and served on a bed of bay leaves.

COTIGNAC

Cotignac Orléanais was made with honey, but this is a modern (and cheaper) version with sugar and oranges.

3.5 kg quinces (in two parcels, one of 2 kg and the other
 of 1.5 kg quinces)
500 g oranges
sugar

Peel 2 kg of the quinces, remove the cores and cut them into segments. Reserve the peel and pips for the second cooking described below.

Put the fruit in a pan and add water until it just covers. Cook for about half an hour until tender. Strain and reserve the cooking water. Press as much pulp as possible through the strainer and keep it to one side.

Put the second batch of fruit, peeled, cored and cut into pieces, into the cooking water reserved from the first batch. Tie all the peels and cores together in a piece of cheese-cloth and put this packet in the pan with the fruit.

Peel the oranges and then section them, removing the pips, pith and membraneous skin as if for a salad. Add them to the quinces in the pan and cook them on a low flame for one hour.

Strain the second batch and add the pulp to the first. At this point, you should weigh the strained fruit and add the same weight in sugar, then boil it down as described in the basic recipe for *membrillo*. Note, you can use the cooking water to make jelly or syrup.

COTOGNATA

This is a Sicilian version, made with the grated flesh of quinces, described by Artusi in his famous *La Scienza in cucina e l'arte di mangiar bene* ('Science in the kitchen and the art of eating well').

Boil quinces in water and take them off the stove when the skins begin to burst.

Remove them from the stove and drain them, take off the peel and grate the fruit ('as best you can', Artusi says) before pressing the flesh through a sieve. Weigh the flesh, add an equal weight of sugar and follow the basic recipe for *membrillo*, above, from this point onwards.

In an Italian cookbook dating from the Middle Ages 'fine spices' are added, such as 'broken cinnamon sticks', with the advice to use sugar rather than honey if the *cotognata* is intended for an invalid.

The realm of fig and quince: Mesopotamia and Persia

Quince: *Beh*
Fig: *Anjir*

> *The Lord shewed me, and, behold, two baskets of figs were set before the temple of the Lord, after that Nebuchadrezzar king of Babylon had carried away captive Jeconiah [...] One basket had very good figs, even like the figs that are first ripe: and the other basket had very naughty figs, which could not be eaten, they were so bad.*
>
> Jeremiah 24:1

In some cultures, recipes have barely changed since antiquity simply because they cannot, or can hardly, be improved. Nowhere is this more true than in Mesopotamia, the Land of Two Rivers, the cradle of agriculture and indeed of our civilization. For millennia it was the centre of food exchange and commerce, the crossroads of caravans from all four quarters. The fertile country itself produced grain, nuts, all sorts of fruit, including citrus fruits, and dates.

In our search for the realm of fig and quince, the Persian kitchen is the first in which we encounter the combination of meat and fruit – dried or fresh – that spread through the culinary cultures of the Middle East and North Africa. A fruit like the quince is particularly well suited to such use because of its hardness and tartness.

Dried fruit like apricots and figs add a delicious exotic accent and the pomegranate occupies a prominent position in Persian cuisine. The use of extracts of rose petals and orange blossoms to perfume desserts and rice dishes evokes a sultry *Arabian Nights* atmosphere. Spinach (*esfenâj*) is a vegetable of Persian origin that is eaten raw or cooked. Another constant item on the Iranian table is yoghurt (*borani*), thick and home-made and excellent for the digestion. The combination of the two, *borani esfenâj*, flavoured with cinnamon and garlic, is a classic.

As far as spices and herbs go, the accent in Persian cooking is on cinnamon and turmeric; it is customary to have a bowl of fresh herbs on the table: mint, tarragon, basil, coriander, parsley, chives, watercress, spring onions and radishes; these are wonderfully refreshing, cleansing the palate and whetting the appetite. Cicero remarked way back in 50 BC that 'the Persians have the lovely habit of eating fresh herbs with bread'.

> *A book of verses underneath the bough*
> *A jug of wine, a loaf of bread – and thou*
> *Beside me singing in the wilderness –*
> *Oh, wilderness were Paradise enow!*
> Rubáiyát of Omar Khayyám (12th century AD)

Arab, Middle Eastern and North African hospitality is justly legendary; even when someone drops by unexpectedly, there must be food, and the table is filled with a wide variety of dishes – from meze to desserts, accompanied by cool lemonade or tea. *Meze* (sometimes *mezze* or *mezeh*) derives from the Persian word *maza*, meaning taste or appetite. A meze consists of a tableful of little dishes with sauces and purées thrilling to the eye and taste buds, made of eggplant, peppers, chick peas, served with raw vegetables, fresh herbs, meat balls, cold meats, fish, olives and fruit, and can be described as a combination of appetizers and snacks, always accompanied by typical white flatbread. Originally intended to mask the sour or bitter taste of unripe wine, these traditional dishes spread westward by way of Turkey to all Mediterranean countries, each of which puts its own stamp on them – as in Spanish *tapas* and Italian *antipasto*. They were even incorporated into meals by non-drinking Muslims.

ABGUSHTE BEH – QUINCE SOUP

500 g lean, boneless lamb
2 onions, minced
60 g yellow split peas (or lentils)
720 ml water
¼ tsp salt
freshly ground black pepper
½ tsp ground turmeric
¼ tsp ground cinnamon
2 tbsp oil (corn or sunflower)
2 quinces, peeled, cored and cut into pieces
2 tbsp lemon juice
pinch of sugar
1 tbsp chopped parsley

Put the lamb with the onions, split peas, water, salt, pepper, turmeric and cinnamon in a pot and bring to a boil. Turn down the heat and leave to simmer for about an hour and a half.

Meanwhile, heat the oil in a frying pan and fry the quinces on low heat until they are soft. Stir in the lemon juice and sugar.

Add the quinces to the soup in the pan and let it cook for another quarter of an hour.

Take the meat from the pan and cut it into small pieces. Sprinkle the parsley on the soup and serve the meat separately with bread, preferably from a Middle

Eastern bakery, with a salad made from spinach, mint and pomegranate seeds, dressed with fragrant olive oil and pomegranate juice.

Whenever fresh quinces are available, you are likely to find fresh pomegranates as well – splendid prehistoric bombs. Select them for weight and colour: the heavier, the juicier, and the redder, the riper and tastier.

Varieties of quince for conserving

Varieties for conserving, mala struthea, cotonea, Scantiana, Scaudiana, orbiculata *and* melimela *(formerly called* mustea*) are all well known to keep if placed on straw in a dry, cool place; therefore those who build fruit stores take care that they face the north, with windows allowing a through draught, but also with shutters, so that if the wind persists the fruit will not lose its juice and begin to shrivel.*

Varro, *On Farming* (1st century BC)

KORESHT-E MORGH

CHICKEN WITH QUINCES AND WALNUT SAUCE

A *koresht* or *goresht* is a dish that is cooked very slowly on a low flame, so that in the end almost all moisture has evaporated – it is something between a stew and a sauce.

> *120 ml corn or sunflower oil*
> *3 onions, thinly sliced*
> *1 kg chicken, jointed*
> *2 quinces, peeled, cored and sliced into segments (to prevent browning, keep in water with lemon juice until used)*
> *250 g walnuts, ground or crushed*
> *300 ml pomegranate juice (or 5 tbsp pomegranate syrup, available in Middle Eastern stores)*
> *2 tsp sugar*
> *salt*

Heat the oil in a large enamelled oven dish and sautée the onion until they begin to change colour. Add the chicken pieces and brown them quickly. Put in the quinces, then add 3 glasses of hot water and turn down the heat. Let simmer softly for half an hour.

Add salt, ground walnuts and pomegranate juice or syrup to the dish. Taste to see if it is too sour and add sugar to taste (syrup already has sugar added).

Simmer everything on low heat until almost all moisture has evaporated. Serve with a fragrant rice such as basmati.

KORESHT-E BEH – LAMB WITH QUINCE

This is a classic Persian dish.

> *500 g boned lamb, cut into cubes*
> *2 onions, thinly sliced*
> *5 tbsp vegetable oil*
> *½ tsp each of ground cinnamon and turmeric*
> *1 tsp salt*
> *¼ tsp black pepper*
> *2 large quinces*
> *3 tbsp sugar*
> *4 tbsp lemon juice*
> *80 g yellow split peas (or lentils)*
> *fresh coriander and/or mint*

Heat the oil in a large oven dish, add the meat and brown it on all sides on high heat. Add the onions and cook until transparent. Sprinkle the cinnamon, turmeric, pepper and salt into the pan and stir well. Pour 240 ml water into the pan and turn the heat to low. Simmer for about an hour, or until the meat is tender.

Wash the down off the quinces, but do not peel them. Remove the cores and cut the quinces into segments. Sautée the quince pieces in a few tablespoons of oil and set aside.

When the meat is tender, add the sugar, lemon juice, split peas and quince. Cover the pan and let everything simmer for another half hour. Serve with rice and fresh coriander and mint.

SHARBAT BEH – QUINCE SYRUP

In the heat of a country like Iran, a guest or a resting caravan is immediately offered a cooling and refreshing drink, which after the introduction of Islam has always been non-alcoholic. This is *panj* (five), the word from which we derive *punch*, which consists of five ingredients: grape juice, rosewater, sugar, lemon or pomegranate juice and ice shavings. *Sharbat*, or sherbet/sorbet, is also a Persian invention – first a drink, then a form of frozen sweetened water. We would call *sharbat* a fruit syrup or lemonade, which can be made sweet or sour, according to taste.

> *2 large quinces*
> *480 ml water*
> *granulated sugar*
> *juice of half a lemon*

Peel the quinces and core them. Chop them into small pieces and just cover them with cold water in a stainless steel or enamelled pan.

Bring slowly to a boil and cook on low heat for about 40 minutes, until the fruit has softened and the flesh has taken on its characteristic orange-pink colour.

Spread out a double layer of cheese-cloth in a deep dish; the cloth should be large enough to hang over the edges of the dish. Pour the fruit and its juice into the dish and close and fasten the cheese-cloth with a piece of string. Raise the cloth with fruit out of the dish and let it drain over the dish for several hours.

Measure the resulting juice and add an equal amount of sugar. Add the lemon juice and bring to a boil. Boil slowly, stirring for about 5 minutes until the sugar has dissolved. Let cool and put into well-rinsed bottles with a screw top.

This syrup can be diluted to make lemonade, or frozen with slightly less water. Stir now and then and freeze it to make a sorbet.

❧ MARINATED FIGS

After the Persian king Xerxes had lost the battle of Salamis to the Greeks in 480 BC, he had fresh figs from Attica served at every meal to help him realize that he did not reign in the country where the figs came from.

Fresh figs should be eaten as simply as possible – at most, sprinkle pomegranate seeds over them for a contrast in texture, marinate them for an hour in orange juice, orange-flower water or Grand Marnier, and dust them with ground cardamom.

To conclude this chapter, I offer a recipe for fig jam – a good way to enjoy a plentiful harvest all year round.

 FIG JAM

> *fresh figs*
> *sugar*
> *grated orange peel*

Cut the stems off the figs. Remove any peel that can be easily pulled off. Weigh the figs and put them in a dish with a little less than their own weight in sugar. A proportion of approximately 750 g sugar to 1 kilo of fruit should work. Let stand overnight.

Next day, put the figs and the sugar in a pan and bring to a boil. Remove the fruit with a slotted spoon as soon as it is boiling and set aside. Add the grated orange peel to the syrup in the pan and let it boil down until the sugar forms pearl-like drops. Add the figs. Cook on low heat for another 15 minutes.

Put the fig jam in clean dry pots and turn them upside down for 5 minutes.

The realm of fig and quince: Turkey

Quince: *Ayva*
Fig: *Incir*

In the early days of the Ottoman Empire, Istanbul – then Constantinople – was a cosmopolitan port with a population of Turks, Greeks, Armenians, Bulgarians, Jews and Arabs, Venetians and Genoese, while cities such as Smyrna (Izmir) and Ephesus (Efes) were important and prosperous trade centres on the Aegean coast from ancient times.

History has supplied Turkish dishes with rich colour and aromas; they represent a confluence of cultures, for which the bridge over the Bosphorus serves as an East-West *trait d'union*. It is striking how many dishes from this melting pot have been given seductive, suggestive names like 'The Sultan's delight', 'The fainting imam', 'Ladies' navels', 'Ladies' thighs' and 'Sweet lips'. This cuisine is also remarkable for its use of nuts and the enticing perfume of rosewater and orange-flower water – as in the famous *loukoum*, or Turkish delight. In an 1862 collection, published in Turkey, of the mainly Ottoman recipes for a banquet on board the Egyptian viceroy's yacht *Faiz-Jehad*, one notes the intensive use of 'cochineal', a natural red colouring made from a dried insect.

Amsterdam began to experience its first influence from Turkish 'guest workers' in the 1960s: Turkish restaurants appeared, with or without belly dancers, like mushrooms from damp ground. Nowadays a Turkish culinary presence in Dutch cities is mostly represented by butchers, who fortunately sell not only meat but spicy olives, *feta* cheese, tea pots and fairy-tale glasses, and as often as not a fine array of fresh vegetables, herbs and fruit, which is often broader, cheaper and fresher than anything you'd find in a supermarket. It is clear that the Turks, even when in 'voluntary exile', stick to their own high standard and style of eating.

This is certainly true of Mustafa Kurt (the surname means 'wolf', a name quite out of keeping with the man's gentle character), who exchanged his Turkish restaurant in Amsterdam for a pizzeria. He says he had to make so many concessions to Dutch tastes that it became impossible for him to serve genuine Turkish food. His menu does not feature figs and quinces, but at home he honours old Turkish traditions. As he talks about his favourite dishes and his birthplace, he gets a nostalgic look in his eyes. When he came to the Netherlands two decades ago with his brothers Mehmet, Ahmet and Hüsnü, they had to leave their parents behind in their native village in Anatolia.

Mustafa shares my fondness for quinces and even eats them raw. The fruit occurs in various Turkish proverbs, he says, and there is a city on the Aegean coast called Ayvalik, which means 'quince orchard'.

Mustafa provided me with several traditional Turkish recipes in this section.

Figs are inseparably linked to Smyrna (Izmir), which is famous for producing the best in Turkey. Turkish cuisine uses them in myriad ways, dried as well as fresh – straight from the tree or at most with a few slices of *feta*. The prophet Muhammed is supposed to have said: 'If I could take a fruit with me to paradise, it would certainly be the fig'.

AYVALI DOLMESI – STUFFED QUINCES

An appetizer for 6 people

> 6 small quinces
> 120 g yellow split peas
> pinch of sugar
> 1 onion, chopped
> 2 tbsp olive oil
> 600 g minced lamb
> 1 tsp tomato paste
> salt, pepper
> pinch of allspice
> 2 tbsp vinegar
> 180 ml chicken stock
> 3 tbsp sugar
> ground cinnamon

Wash the split peas and boil them in 480 ml of lightly sugared water for 45 minutes, until cooked. Drain them.

In the meantime, cut the tops off the quinces and carefully hollow them out. Cut the removed flesh in cubes and keep the tops.

Heat the olive oil in a frying pan and sautée the chopped onion, the quince cubes, the strained cooked split peas and the minced meat for about ten minutes, until the meat is no longer red. Add the tomato paste and season with salt and freshly ground black pepper. Continue frying for a few more minutes while stirring.

Fill the hollowed-out quinces with the mixture and put the tops back on.

Mix the vinegar with the stock and the sugar and a little cinnamon and bring everything to a boil. Preheat the oven to 180°C.

Pour the stock into an oven dish in which the quinces fit snugly and put the quinces in side by side. Cover the whole with a piece of foil and put the dish in the oven until the quinces are cooked, about 45 minutes to one hour.

Tall thriving trees confessed the fruitful mould;
The reddening apple ripens here to gold,
Here the blue fig with luscious juice o'erflows,
With deeper red the full pomegranate glows,
The branch here bends beneath the weighty pear,
And verdant olives flourish round the year.
The balmy spirit of the western gale
Eternal breathes on fruits untaught to fail:
Each dropping pear a following pear supplies,
On apples apples, figs on figs arise:
The same mild season gives the blooms to blow,
The buds to harden, and the fruits to grow.

Alexander Pope, after Homer

PILAV AYVALI KABAK KESTANELI
PILAF WITH QUINCES, PUMPKIN AND CHESTNUTS

Three autumn fruits combined to make a simple, nutritious dish. *Pilaf* is the Turkish word for rice, which in the Middle East is usually first fried, then cooked with a variety of other ingredients mixed in.

Buy fresh chestnuts that are shiny and don't rattle. Carve a cross in them and cook them in water or roast them in the oven for 20–40 minutes. Startle them with cold water and peel them. You can also buy canned chestnuts (make sure they are unsweetened, at least for this dish), and around the December holidays, you can often find vacuum-packed cooked and peeled chestnuts imported from France. This will serve between 6 and 8 people.

240 g basmati rice
240 g bulghur wheat
25 g butter
1.5 tbsp olive oil
2 minced onions
1 clove of garlic, minced
1 large quince
300 g pumpkin, peeled and cubed
300 g chestnuts, peeled, halved and cooked
960 ml water or chicken or lamb stock
salt, pepper, pinch of ground cinnamon
1 lemon
fresh coriander leaves for garnishing

Heat the butter and oil in a large pan with a thick bottom and sautée the onion and garlic until soft. Do not let the garlic burn or it will get bitter.

Wash the down off the quince, quarter it, remove the core and cut it into small pieces; there is no need to peel it. Add the pieces to the onion and sautée them on low heat. Add the pumpkin and chestnuts. Add more oil if necessary and fry everything for 10 more minutes on low heat.

Now add the rice and bulghur and fry everything for another 5 minutes, while stirring constantly. Season with salt and pepper and add a pinch of cinnamon.

Bring the stock or water to a boil, pour it over the pilaf, stir well and let it cook on a very low heat for 20 minutes. Squeeze the lemon over the dish before serving and garnish with fresh coriander leaves.

It is possible to cook a *pilaf* in the oven, a method that avoids any danger of burning or sticking to the pan. If you use an ovenproof casserole, do the preliminary frying on the top, add the stock and finish in a medium oven for 15 minutes. Test the rice for tenderness, then fork it through to separate the grains.

BÀLIK AYVALI – FISH WITH QUINCES IN FILO PASTRY

We have now reached the sea on our journey, so it is time for fish! This dish can be made with any kind of white fish fillet, but sea bass is tastiest. It always takes a little time to make pastry parcels, but these are well worth the effort. The only thing you need to accompany this dish is a fresh green salad with lots of fresh herbs.

> *according to taste and size 1 or 2 fish fillets per person*
> *1 packet of filo pastry*
> *1 or 2 quinces, peeled and cored*
> *leaves of a sturdy kind of lettuce, like romaine*
> *lemon juice*

Grease a large flat oven tray or dish with olive oil. Preheat the oven to 180°C.

Prepare the filo dough according to the instructions on the packet. Slice the quinces as thinly as possible. First put a salad leaf on the buttered pastry sheet, then a layer of thinly sliced quince, then the fish fillet and then another layer of quince. Sprinkle with lemon juice.

Fold the pastry into packets. Pinch the edges, brush them with butter and put them in the oiled oven dish.

Bake them in the oven for 30 to 40 minutes, depending on the kind of fish and the thickness of the fillets. If the pastry browns too quickly, before the fish is done, cover the oven tray with a sheet of aluminium foil to prevent further burning.

HOSHAF – COMPOTE OF DRIED FRUIT

This is a traditional dish for weddings and parties. It is richer than the 'tutti frutti' which has now gone out of fashion. For an especially festive touch, you can add a dash of your own favourite eau-de-vie or liqueur at the last minute. Lemon and/or orange peel also enhances the flavour.

> *225 g sugar*
> *1 litre water*
> *100 g dried apricots*
> *100 g dried, pitted prunes*
> *100 g raisins*
> *100 g dried figs*
> *225 g mixed nuts, such as blanched almonds, pistachio nuts, walnuts*
> *dash of liqueur or eau-de-vie; orange or lemon peel (optional)*

Dissolve the sugar in the water and boil for 5 minutes. Add the dried fruit. Stirring, cook on low heat for about 15 minutes.

Stir in the nuts. Heat thoroughly for 5 minutes and let the compote cool. It is best served at room temperature.

The realm of fig and quince: Greece and Greek Cyprus

Quince: *Kydonia*
Fig: *Syko*

> *To left and right, outside, he saw an orchard*
> *Closed by a pale – four spacious acres planted*
> *With trees in bloom or weighted down for picking:*
> *Pear trees, pomegranates, brilliant apples,*
> *Luscious figs, and olives ripe and dark.*
>
> Homer, *The Odyssey*

In Greece we arrive in the mythical realm of the quince, which owes its name to the city of Kythonia, now Chaniá, on the island of Crete. Cyprus, which for convenience's sake I count as part of Greece and not Turkey, has a quince story as well: it is where, according to myth, Aphrodite or Venus, goddess of the golden apples, arrived after her birth from the waves (in Petra tou Romiu, Aphrodite's Rock at Paphos). In Kouklia, about fifteen kilometres south of Paphos – initially the name for the whole island, later only the old port city went by this name – a temple dedicated to Aphrodite was excavated.

The fig already enjoyed great popularity in antiquity;

every citizen of Athens, including Plato, was a *philosykos*, a friend of figs. Mithridates, king of Pontus (132–63 BC), praised them as a remedy for numerous illnesses, told his doctors to prescribe them frequently and urged his subjects to eat them daily. Olympic athletes followed a fig diet when in training.

Greek cuisine is fairly well known, be it from restaurants or from holidays. One thinks of lamb roasted on a charcoal fire, the intoxicating scent of oregano, both in the kitchen and along walking trails on the Greek islands. With lemon, these form the trinity that is the foundation of Hellenic flavour.

Because Greece has so much coastline, fish cannot be ignored. Fish, like figs, profits from a minimum of additions and is best grilled fresh from the sea. That way you don't even need extra salt.

One of the oldest texts on food we have dates from about 330 BC, written by Archestratus, a Greek living in Sicily whose life seems to have consisted of travelling and eating, and who reported on both in verse. Much of his 'gastronomic poetry' has been lost, but what we have we owe to Athenaeus (around 200 AD), who quoted him extensively in his *Deipnosophistae* (The Banquet of Scholars). To eat bonito (a relative of the mackerel) at its best, Archestratus said, you must wrap it in fig leaves with a few sprigs of oregano and broil it in hot ashes.

Let us begin with an idyllic dinner on one of the Greek islands. The table has been set under a fig tree, from which we pick some leaves and sun-warmed figs. The oregano can't be too far away. The fire is stoked while we start with the *sykosalata* (fig salad) described below. When the coals have gone grey all over, the fish is wrapped in fig leaves with oregano and laid in the ashes to broil. The coffee after the meal is made 'à la Turque', flavoured with cardamom and accompanied by a dish of Greek yoghurt with baked quinces or a few tablespoons of quince jelly stirred in.

 HIRINO ME KYTHONIA – PORK WITH QUINCES

> *'Dear Pig, are you willing to sell for one shilling*
> *Your ring?' Said the Piggy, 'I will.'*
> *So they took it away, and were married next day*
> *By the Turkey who lives on the hill.*
> *They dined on mince and slices of quince,*
> *Which they ate with a runcible spoon.*
> Edward Lear, 'The Owl and the Pussycat'

There are many versions of this dish; this one was given to me by a Greek lady on the island of Rhodes.

1 kg boneless pork, cut into cubes
30 g butter, 2 tbsp olive oil
300 ml red wine

150 ml water
lemon peel
pinch of ground cinnamon
salt, pepper
1 kg quinces
30 g brown sugar
fresh or dried marjoram or oregano for garnishing

Heat the butter and the oil in a large casserole and brown the meat. Add all other ingredients except the quinces and sugar. Lower the heat and let the meat simmer for one hour.

Peel and core the quinces. Cut them into thick slices, put them in a dish and sprinkle them with the brown sugar. Set aside while the meat is cooking.

Arrange the quince slices on top of the meat in the pan and let everything stew for another hour. Shake the pan from time to time instead of stirring, which might break up the fruit. Sprinkle liberally with marjoram or oregano just before serving with rice.

🖎 *YAOURTI ME KYTHANIA* – YOGHURT WITH QUINCES

> *500 g quinces*
> *100 g sugar*
> *200 ml water*
> *60 ml lemon juice*
> *300 ml plain Greek yoghurt*
> *2 tbsp (Greek) honey*
> *grated peel of half a lemon*

Peel and core the quinces; save peel and cores. Cut the fruit in slices.

Put the water in a pan with the sugar and lemon juice and stir over medium heat until the sugar has dissolved.

Put the peel and cores in the syrup and let simmer for 20 minutes, until it has reduced somewhat. Strain through a sieve and return to the pan.

Put the quince slices in the syrup and poach them gently until cooked, about 15 minutes.

Leave the fruit to cool in the syrup.

Stir the honey and lemon peel into the yoghurt.

Serve the quince in syrup in individual bowls and top with the aromatic yoghurt.

❧ *SYKOSALATA* – FIG SALAD

> *2 or 3 fresh ripe figs per person*
> feta *or another sheep's or goat's milk cheese*
> *bunch of fresh oregano and/or basil*
> *cayenne pepper, ground*
> *olive oil (extra virgin)*
> *juice of 1 small orange*

Cut the stems off the figs, wash the fruit and cut them into segments. The peel of most figs can be eaten, but if it feels too leathery you can easily pull it off. Arrange the pieces on a pretty plate or dish.

Cut the cheese into cubes and add to the figs. The proportions can be determined by personal taste; the salad is especially luxurious when the figs dominate.

Tear the leaves from four or five sprigs of herbs and add to the plate of figs and cheese. Sprinkle a pinch of cayenne pepper over the whole.

Dress the salad with a fragrant, fruity extra virgin olive oil mixed with orange juice (3 parts oil to 1 part juice). Add a little sea salt if the cheese is not too salty.

TOURTA ME SYKO – CAKE WITH YOGHURT AND FIGS

At first glance one might not want to cover soft fresh figs in batter, but in this upside-down cake nothing of their delicate flavour is lost.

> *3 tbsp mild honey*
> *200 g softened butter*
> *175 g light brown sugar*
> *grated peel of 1 lemon*
> *grated peel of 1 orange*
> *4 eggs, separated*
> *225 g flour*
> *1 tsp baking powder*
> *1 tsp baking soda*
> *250 ml plain Greek yoghurt*

Preheat the oven to 180°C. Cover the bottom of a 23-centimetre cake tin with a sheet of baking parchment. In a tin with an non-stick layer one can do without the paper, but in both cases the tin should be lightly buttered. Cut the figs into slices, arrange then in a nice pattern on the paper and brush them lightly with honey.

Beat the butter with the sugar and grated peel to an airy, light mixture. Stir in the egg yolks one by one.

Sift the flour with the baking powder and soda into a separate bowl and alternately add yoghurt and the butter-sugar mixture; stir until it becomes a homogenous batter.

Beat the egg whites in another bowl to stiff peaks. First fold one half of the egg whites into the cake batter and then carefully fold in the rest.

Cover the figs with the cake batter and bake the cake in the oven for one hour. It is done when a toothpick stuck into the centre comes out clean.

Let the cake cool for 15 minutes before turning it upside down onto a plate. Drizzle some honey over it before serving.

Photograph: Clare Pawley.

The realm of fig and quince: Italy

Quince: *Mela cotogna*
Fig: *Fico*

> *If you tell me that you require a fig,*
> *I answer you that there must be time.*
> *Let it first blossom, then bear fruit, then ripen.*
>
> Epictetus (AD 55–135)

The best and most relaxed way to travel from Greece to Italy is by boat, from Piraeus through the Strait of Messina to Naples. We now leave the Middle East behind but linger a little while with the goats and their shepherd in the shade of fig trees.

In Italy there are many goat's and sheep's milk cheeses, like *pecorino*, which are sharp and excellently suited to being combined with figs as well as quinces. Of course, there is also soft cheese, the best-known kind being the southern *mozzarella di buffalo*, which is sadly never at its best outside its native region – it should really be no more than a day old.

When I once spent several months on Procida, the smallest island in the Gulf of Naples, I was awoken the first morning by a typical Italian sound: a scooter's sputtering.

I looked out of the window and saw a scene straight out of a Vittorio de Sica movie: something between a scooter and a bicycle cart, the Italian equivalent of a rickshaw often used as a taxi in the south, had parked in the street below. People were flocking to it (it was seven in the morning) and going away holding what looked like a boiled egg or a whole bag of boiled eggs. It was only the next day that I recovered from my culinary jetlag and realized these were balls of mozzarella. The cart carrying fresh wares arrived every day by boat from Pozzuoli and the villages in the Naples hinterland where the buffalo roam. If you serve older mozzarella you are looked at askance. At most the cheese is then used for pizza, with nothing more than a clutch of basil.

The fig's classic significant other is *prosciutto di Parma*. Figs are also dried in Italy; in Bari on the Adriatic coast they add almonds, fennel seeds and bay leaves for an especially fragrant flavour.

Mosaics and murals from Pompeii show that the quince was also prized in ancient Roman times. Pliny the Elder, one of the victims of the famous eruption of Vesuvius (and of his own curiosity, because he went there to study the phenomenon), gave the fruit elaborate attention in his wonderful *Natural History*. In the same way as we can read in Apicius' *De Re Coquinaria*, he described a method for enlarging a pig's liver before slaughter by feeding it dried figs and giving it mead to drink. Such a liver was called *fictatum*.

The quince occurs in the famous banquet of Trimalchio, described by Petronius in the first century AD, and on the menu of a banquet given by Pope Pius V in 1570. A quince pie was served on the latter occasion, with the special note that a whole fruit was to be used per head.

First I will give the recipes for several sauces which can be served either with roasted meat or poultry or on bread with an Italian cheese – gorgonzola, Parmigiano, pecorino, taleggio, even mozzarella or ricotta. The first is a '*mostarda di frutta*' which, according to Elizabeth David, dates from antiquity and in northern provinces is also sometimes eaten with river fish or eel.

MOSTARDA DI COTOGNA – QUINCE MUSTARD

This closely resembles a relish or chutney and is used in the same way. It is usually made with a mixture of fruits in a thickened sweet-and-sour syrup with herbs and/or spices. For the Italian *mostardas* – those of Venice and Cremona being the most celebrated – there are various methods of preparation: with sugar or honey; with mustard oil, powder or seed; with wine or with water. It is, in a manner of speaking, Liberty Hall, and each cook can make his or her mark on the recipe. Here are two of mine.

Quince *mostarda* is a speciality of the northern Italian town of Vicenza. Elizabeth David tells of visiting Venice in the autumn and finding it on sale to families whose eager purchases would ensure that stocks were exhausted by Christmas.

QUINCE MUSTARD (1)

> *480 g peeled and chopped quince*
> *60 g ground mustard seed*
> *600 ml dry white wine*
> *the zested peel of 2 oranges*
> *360 ml cider vinegar*
> *360 g sugar, either white or brown*
> *1 tbsp salt*
> *pinch of allspice*
> *pinch of ground cinnamon*
> *juice of half a lemon*

Put all the ingredients except the lemon juice in a pan with a heavy bottom, bring to a boil while stirring and let simmer on very low heat for an hour to an hour and a half, until thickened. Stir regularly, especially the last half hour, so that the mixture does not stick to the pan.

Remove the pan from the cooker and stir in the lemon juice. Let the *mostarda* cool and put it in clean jars. Seal and keep cool.

QUINCE MUSTARD (2)

750 g quinces
250 g dried figs
720 g honey
1 lemon
120 g whole mustard seeds
240 ml dry white wine

Cut the fruit into small pieces and put it just under water in a thick-bottomed pan. Add 1 tablespoon of honey and the grated peel of a lemon.

Cook the fruit for 30 minutes on medium heat without cover. Stir from time to time. Let cool.

Warm the wine in another pan with the rest of the honey. Boil the syrup down to a third of its volume and stir in the mustard seeds. Let cool.

Mix the fruit mixture with the honey syrup, put in preserving jars and let the *mostarda* thicken in the fridge.

SALSA DI FICHI CON ACETO BALSAMICO
FIG SAUCE WITH BALSAMIC VINEGAR

Few food items have been so in vogue during the last decade as balsamic vinegar – and it has gone from being a fashion product to being a fixture of most pantries. Its history can be traced back to Columbus: among the many novelties and souvenirs he brought back from his second journey to the New World were a few cuttings of the balsam pine (*Abies balsamea*), which has since flourished in southern Europe. The wood is mainly used in Italy to make barrels in which the extraordinarily mild vinegar made from the white Trebbiano grape is ripened. It is the oily, aromatic resin in the balsam wood that gives the Modena vinegar its distinctive aroma and flavour, and the rule is that the longer it is left to mature in the barrels, the fuller and smoother it gets. As with wine there are balsamic vinegars with an 'appellation contrôlée', a denomination of origin and vintage, and some bottles come with a price tag of more than 100 Euros.

500 g fresh figs
80 ml red wine
3 tbsp balsamic vinegar
salt, pepper
½ tsp sugar or honey
2 twigs of fresh thyme

Put all the ingredients in a pan with half a cup of water. Cover with a lid and bring to a boil. Turn down the heat and keep the pan half covered by the lid. Cook slowly for about half an hour.

Remove the thyme twigs and press the mixture through a coarse sieve with a wooden spoon, or use a food mill if you find that easier.

 POLENTA CON FICHI E MASCARPONE
POLENTA WITH FIGS AND MASCARPONE

A breakfast that will keep you going until it's time for *antipasti*.

> *960 ml milk*
> *240 g coarse instant polenta*
> *30 g butter*
> *60 ml honey*
> *4 tbsp* mascarpone
> *4 large fresh figs, cut into segments*

Bring the milk to a boil and stir in the polenta. Reduce the heat to low and keep stirring until the polenta is creamy, about 2 minutes.

Stir in the butter and the *mascarpone*. Put the fig segments on top and drizzle with honey.

Three salads with figs and (goat's) cheese follow, intended as lunch or starter dishes.

INSALATA DI FICHI E MOZZARELLA
FIG AND MOZZARELLA SALAD

> *8 fresh figs*
> *2 mozzarellas, preferably buffalo*
> *1 tbsp walnut oil*
> *2 tbsp olive oil*
> *1 lemon*
> *1 clove of garlic, crushed*
> *10 basil leaves*
> *salt, pepper*

Slice the mozzarella thinly and arrange on a plate.

Mix the two oils, the crushed garlic, the juice of the lemon and the salt and pepper.

Pour the dressing on the mozzarella and let it marinate in the fridge for 1 hour or more. Turn the slices over several times.

Wash the figs and slice them crosswise into rounds. Arrange the mozzarella and figs alternately on a serving plate and pour the dressing over them. Grind some fresh black pepper over them and garnish with the basil.

INSALATA STROMBOLI – STROMBOLI SALAD

The story goes that during the filming of *Stromboli* (1950), Ingrid Bergman and Roberto Rossellini confirmed the truth of the notion that the quickest way to the heart is through the stomach, while eating the following salad.

> *2 red peppers*
> *12 anchovies*
> *2 potatoes, boiled in their skins*
> *half a fennel bulb*
> *6 fresh ripe figs*
> *2 tbsp capers*
> *2 sprigs mint*
> *olive oil*
> *pepper*

Roast the capsicums until the skin begins to blister. Put them in a bowl and cover the bowl with clingfilm. Let the peppers cool for half an hour, until they are cool enough to handle. Peel them and cut them into strips.

Drain the anchovies and peel the potatoes. Cut the potatoes in thin slices and the anchovies into pieces. Wash the fennel, remove the outer stalks if necessary and cut the bulb into slices.

Wash the figs and cut them into segments.

Arrange the potato, fennel and figs on a plate. Put the peppers and anchovies on top, together with the capers and some of their juice. Sprinkle with mint leaves.

Put the plate in the fridge for a few hours to let the flavours mingle and sprinkle with olive oil just before serving. The anchovies make extra salt superfluous, but do add black pepper to taste.

 INSALATA DI RUCOLA CON FICHI – ROCKET SALAD WITH FIGS

> *1 bunch of rocket*
> *1 small melon*
> *10 ripe figs*
> *2 tbsp pine nuts*
> *the grated zest of half an orange*
> *the juice of an orange*
> *salt*
> *approx. 3 tbsp olive oil*

Wash the rocket and put it in a bowl.

Cut the melon in pieces and the figs into segments or slices.

Brown the pine nuts lightly in olive oil, sprinkle them on the figs together with the orange peel.

Make a dressing with the olive oil and orange juice and serve it on the side.

CAVOLO CON FINOCCHIO E COTOGNA
SAVOY CABBAGE WITH FENNEL AND QUINCE

This recipe is from a medieval 'Libro della Cocina', author unknown.

> *half a Savoy cabbage, shredded*
> *1 onion, sliced*
> *1 fennel bulb, sliced*
> *5 tbsp olive oil*
> *1 quince, peeled and chopped, set aside in 120 ml water*
>   *or stock with lemon juice*
> *100 g* prosciutto *(Italian raw ham) or* pancetta
>   *(Italian spiced bacon), cut into strips*

Blanch the cabbage in boiling water for 2 minutes and drain.

Heat the olive oil and sautée the onion and fennel until they soften, 5 to 10 minutes.

Add the cabbage and quince, with water or stock, to the pan and let simmer until almost all the moisture has evaporated. Season with salt and pepper.

Fry the *prosciutto* or *pancetta* in one tablespoon of olive oil and stir into the cabbage mixture just before serving.

FETTUCINE CON FICHI E GORGONZOLA
FETTUCINE WITH FIGS AND GORGONZOLA SAUCE

A visit to Italy must include at least one pasta dish. *Ecco!*

>*2 tsp light olive oil*
>*160 g spring onions, chopped*
>*2 shallots, chopped*
>*120 ml dry white wine*
>*240 ml cream*
>*70 g gorgonzola, crumbled*
>*8 fresh firm figs, quartered*
>*2 tbsp fresh basil leaves*
>*400 g tomato, peeled and chopped*
>*500 g pasta*
>*salt, pepper*
>*freshly grated parmesan*

Put a large pan of salted water to boil for the pasta. In the meantime heat the oil in a large frying pan and fry the onion and shallots until transparent. Pour in the wine and let it reduce for 1 or 2 minutes. Then add the cream and let it boil for another minute. Turn down the heat and add the crumbled gorgonzola. Stir the sauce until the cheese has melted.

Add the figs, basil and 325 g of the tomato to the pan and let cook until heated through. Turn off the heat and let the sauce rest, covered.

Cook the pasta *al dente* and strain.

Stir the pasta into the sauce or serve separately, with the rest of the tomato and freshly grated Parmesan.

CROSTATA DI COTOGNA – QUINCE PIE

> *200 g quince*
> *red wine, sugar*
> *150 g softened butter*
> *100 g self-raising flour*
> *200 g plain flour*
> *3 egg yolks*
> *150 g sugar*
> *juice and peel of 1 lemon*
> *1 whisked egg*

Peel the quince, remove the core and cut into thin slices. Put the slices in red wine to cover, add a few teaspoons of sugar and boil. The fruit should not disintegrate, so keep an eye on it. When tender, strain the slices and put them aside.

Rub the butter into the two kinds of flour in a bowl.

Beat the egg yolks with the sugar and add to the flour mixture, together with the lemon juice and peel. Mix well. This dough can be made in a food processor.

Wrap the dough in clingfilm and put it in the fridge for at least one hour. Preheat the oven to 180°C.

Grease a pie tin with butter, roll out the dough and cover the bottom of the tin with it. If you wish you can reserve one-third of the dough to make a decoration on top of the filling. Arrange the quince slices on top of the dough and brush with egg.

Bake the *crostata* for 40 minutes, or until brown.

FICHI AL VINO CON SCHIUMA DI MASCARPONE
FIGS IN WINE WITH MASCARPONE FOAM

A scrumptious and heady pudding for 6 people.

18 fresh figs
the juice and grated zest of 2 oranges
the juice and grated zest of 2 lemons
1 bottle red wine
200 g sugar
1 stick cinnamon
1 vanilla bean, split open

for the *mascarpone* foam
500 g mascarpone
125 g sugar
2 eggs, separated
140 ml grappa

Wash the figs and put them in a pan in which they fit snugly. Sprinkle the sugar and grated orange and lemon peel over the figs.

Pour the wine and the juice of the lemons and oranges over the figs. Add the cinnamon and vanilla and bring gradually to the boil. Turn down the heat and let simmer for about half an hour, uncovered. Shake the pan gently now and then, so the fruit doesn't stick to the bottom.

Remove the figs with a slotted spoon and arrange them in a serving dish. Boil down the wine on high heat until syrupy; remove the cinnamon and vanilla and pour the sauce over the figs. Let cool in the fridge. Serve the figs with a topping of *mascarpone* foam.

Put the cheese in a bowl with the sugar and beat until light and frothy.

Beat in the egg yolks one by one and then add the grappa.

Beat the egg whites until very stiff and fold them into the *mascarpone*, carefully but thoroughly. Let the foam stiffen for a few hours in the fridge before serving.

He am I of the fruit of the bad garden,
Who here a date am getting for my fig.
Dante, *Inferno*, translated by Longfellow

The realm of fig and quince: France

Quince: *Coing*
Fig: *Figue*

That strange man Nostradamus ensured that the quince, which he considered 'un trésor des bienfaits' (a treasure of blessings), acquired a substantial reputation beyond Orléans, the city known for its *cotignac*.

Michel de Nostre-Dame was (in all likelihood) born in December 1503 in Saint-Rémy-de-Provence, north-east of Arles, and became a gifted physician and astrologer, professions which in those days went hand in hand. He was a proponent of combining business with pleasure and was one of the first to use sugar in his practice, in fruit jams and jellies or syrups, with or without spices like ginger and cloves.

In the Musée d'Art Chrétien in Arles one can admire the quinces and figs that adorn the fruit garlands carved on ancient tombstones from the Roman cemetery of Alyscamps.

I read in a French book on wild food: 'The fig tree is like the *pastis*: despite its southern associations you come across it everywhere.' The fig has led French *haute cuisine* chefs to invent the most decadent delicacies, among which the fig dipped in hot chocolate seems to me the most misconceived. However, Escoffier understood figs

and restrained himself. He 'merely' marinated them in
Grand Marnier or Cointreau and added dots of whipped
cream before serving them. My own finishing touch is a
pinch of cardamom.

ANCHOÏADE DE FIGUES, FRITURE DE CREVETTES
ANCHOVY AND FIG SAUCE WITH FRIED SHRIMP

Anchoïade, a Corsican speciality, is often recommended to
serve with cooked fish, but it is also an excellent dipping
sauce for fried battered shrimp. This dish depends entirely
on the quality of the anchovies; do not buy the canned
variety, but the little glass jars imported from France or
Italy with anchovies preserved in olive oil or salt. 'Anchois
de Collioure' are delicious and never assault the taste buds.
At all event, rinse the anchovies in cold water before use.
Choose prawns (scampi or gambas), they are larger and
easier to handle that the tiny North Sea shrimp.

50 g anchovies
1 red pepper
50 g blanched almonds
90 ml olive oil
2 cloves of garlic
5 dried figs
2 tbsp lemon juice
1 tsp fennel seed
freshly ground black pepper
400 g prawns

for the shrimp batter
60 g flour
1 tbsp olive oil
pinch of salt
approx. 120 ml warm water
2 egg whites

Make the sauce first. Grill or roast the pepper in the flame of a grill, or in the oven until the skin starts to blister. Let it cool in a bowl covered with clingfilm then peel it.

Cut the stems off the figs, peel the garlic and put them in a food processor together with the rinsed, dried anchovies, the pepper, almonds, fennel seeds and lemon juice. Process everything coarsely. Slowly add the olive oil while the machine is running until it is a homogenous sauce. Season with black pepper (no salt is needed on account of the anchovies), a drop of lemon juice to taste and, if the sauce is too thick, with a little more olive oil.

Mix all the batter ingredients except the egg whites and set aside for at least one hour. Beat the egg whites stiff just before you are going to fry the prawns and fold them into the batter.

Precook the prawns by sweating them to a nice pale pink on low heat in a frying pan without fat or water. Shake the pan now and then. Peel the prawns as soon as they are cold enough to handle.

Dip the prawns in batter and fry them in hot olive oil. Serve with the anchoïade on the side.

ॐ *COINGS ET CHAMPIGNONS SAUVAGES AU FOUR*
OVEN-BAKED QUINCE WITH WILD MUSHROOMS

A very tasty appetizer or first course in the season when the *cep* or penny bun, the most cuddly of wild mushrooms, raises its irresistible fleshy head. It can also be made with dried *ceps* or *porcini*, or even cultivated portobellos or oyster mushrooms.

> *2 quinces*
> *juice of 1 ½ lemons*
> *180 ml Madeira*
> *salt, pepper*
> *250 g fresh or 25 g dried mushrooms*
> *2 tbsp butter*
> *1 small onion, chopped*
> *leaves stripped off 2 twigs of thyme, plus a few sprigs for*
>   *the finish*

Preheat the oven to 180°C. Cut the quinces in half, remove the cores carefully and put the fruit in an oven dish with their cut surface upwards. Anoint them with the lemon juice to prevent browning. Sprinkle the fruit with a little of the Madeira and add some salt and pepper.

Add a cup of water to the dish, then cover it with aluminium foil. Bake this in a moderate oven for 1 hour.

Brush or rub clean the mushrooms; chop them coarsely. If you are using dried mushrooms, soak them for 10 minutes in hot water. Squeeze the moisture from them and save it.

Heat the butter in a frying pan and fry the onions for a few minutes until transparent. Add the mushrooms and the thyme and cook them, stirring all the while, until the mushrooms begin to soften, about 10 minutes. Pour the rest of the Madeira (and when appropriate the water from soaking dried mushrooms) into this pan and season with salt and pepper. Boil to reduce the liquid in the pan to about half.

Ladle the mushrooms over the quinces, let everything get heated through and garnish the dish with sprigs of thyme.

PINTADE AU COINGS – GUINEA FOWL WITH QUINCES

Quinces combine well with poultry or game. Guinea fowl, even when farmed, has a pleasant, mildly wild flavour. In French, it owes its name to the word *peindre*, to paint, as in *oiseau peint*, painted bird, for its lovely plumage which looks as if it has been painted with a fine brush.

1 guinea fowl (750 g to 1.3 kg)
2 tbsp butter
2 quinces
2 or 3 tbsp honey
160 ml cider or apple juice
75 ml single cream

Preheat the oven to 180°C. Put the fowl in a buttered oven dish and rub it all over with butter. Peel and core the quinces and put the peel and cores inside the bird. Cover the breast with buttered baking parchment.

Cut the quince into pieces and add honey and cider. Put the mixture around the guinea fowl.

Put the dish in the oven and bake it for about one hour to one hour and a half. If you prick the thigh the juices running out should be clear. About halfway through cooking, take off the baking parchment and then baste the bird from time to time with honey and more cider.

CÔTELETTES D'AGNEAU AUX FIGUES ET ROMARIN
LAMB CHOPS WITH FIGS AND ROSEMARY

> *2 or 3 lamb chops per person*
> *12 fresh figs*
> *2 tbsp sugar*
> *3 or 4 sprigs of rosemary*
> *250 ml red wine*
> *olive oil*
> *salt and pepper*

Preheat the oven to 180°C. Wash the figs and cut them in half. Put them in an oven dish, sprinkle with half the rosemary (the needles stripped from the twigs) and 2 tablespoons of sugar; pour in the wine, diluted with 80 ml water. Put the dish uncovered in the oven and let the figs bake for 20 minutes. Remove the figs from their cooking liquid and if necessary reduce the wine a little.

Fry the lamb chops in hot olive oil with the rest of the rosemary to the desired degree of doneness (they should still be pink in the middle). Sprinkle with sea salt and black pepper and arrange the figs around the lamb before serving. Anoint with the sauce, which you should check for seasoning.

These baked figs can also be served with a roast leg of lamb.

🍀 *VIN DE FIGUE* – FIG WINE

Without wine we wouldn't really be in France. Recently, remains of fig wine have been found in ancient amphoras.

Put 1 kg of figs in 10 litres of water. Add some juniper berries. Let stand for seven days. Decant into bottles that can be sealed hermetically. Let stand another seven days; this wine can be drunk with one of the following desserts.

🍀 *GRATIN DE FIGUES* – FIG GRATIN

> *1 fig per person*
> *2 egg yolks*
> *2 egg shells of sugar*
> *4 egg shells white wine*
> *(use the shells from the eggs as a measuring cup)*

Cut the figs into segments and arrange them in a buttered, fireproof dish.

Mix the egg yolks with the sugar and wine in a sauce pan. Bring slowly up to heat while whisking. The mixture will thicken slightly. Do not boil. It may be safer and less worrisome to do this in a double-boiler.

Pour the egg mixture over the figs and put it under a hot grill for about 5 minutes until set and lightly browned.

FIGUES FARCIS, GLACE À L'HUILE D'OLIVE
STUFFED FIGS, OLIVE OIL ICE-CREAM

> for the figs
> *8 fresh figs, as large as possible*
> *50 g honey*
> *½ tsp fennel seeds*
> *250 ml sweet red wine*
> *250 ml whipping cream*
> quatr'épices, *a mixture of nutmeg, white pepper, cloves*
>   *and ginger or cinnamon*
> *1 tbsp raspberry jam*
>
> for the ice-cream
> *500 ml milk*
> *250 ml crème fraîche*
> *150 g sugar*
> *5 egg yolks*
> *100 ml olive oil (sweet and fragrant, extra virgin)*
> *1 vanilla bean*

Wash the figs, prick them all over with a fork and put them in a pan with the honey, wine and fennel seeds. Slowly bring them to a boil. Turn down the heat and let them simmer for two minutes. Let them cool in the syrup.

Remove the figs from the syrup and cut off their tops. Carefully spoon out the flesh and put it in a bowl. Beat the cream to thicken it and add it to the fruit with the *quatr'épices* and the raspberry jam. Mix well.

Stuff the figs with the cream mixture and put the tops back on. Let them cool thoroughly in the fridge.

Reduce the syrup and serve it separately.

To make the ice-cream, heat the milk and the cream with the vanilla. Beat the egg yolks and the sugar until light and fluffy. Remove the pan from the heat and stir the hot cream mixture into the yolks.

Put the pan back on low heat and stir until the mixture thickens and sticks to the spoon. Do not boil.

Pour in the olive oil and put the mixture in an ice-cream maker. Follow the instructions. If you don't possess an ice-cream machine, stir up the ice-cream three times while it is freezing, so it becomes airy.

ॐ *SORBET DE COINGS* – QUINCE SORBET

> *2 quinces*
> *2 tbsp brandy*
> *500 g sugar*

Peel and core the quinces and quarter them. Put them in a pan with the brandy and about 240 ml of water. Put a lid on the pan and let the quinces simmer until they are soft, while stirring occasionally. Depending on the size and type of fruit this can take from 15 to 40 minutes. Let the fruit cool and purée it in a food processor or press it through a sieve.

In another pan bring 240 ml water to a boil with the sugar. Stir well until the sugar has dissolved. Let cool.

Mix 1 ½ cups quince purée with two-thirds of a cup of sugar syrup. Freeze it in an ice-cream maker or put it in ice-cube trays. If the latter, the sorbet should be stirred three times with a fork while it is freezing.

CHARLOTTE AU CHOCOLAT ET AUX COINGS
CHARLOTTE WITH CHOCOLATE AND QUINCES

Our last French dessert is a knock-out. You will need a special charlotte tin, or a cake tin with sides as tall as a sponge finger biscuit. If you can't lay your hands on one, cut the biscuits to fit your own cake tin.

750 ml water
1 vanilla bean
275 g powdered sugar
3 quinces
200 g good quality dark chocolate
6 eggs, separated
approx. 24 sponge fingers

Bring the water to a boil with 75 g sugar and the vanilla (split open and the seeds scraped out).

Peel and core the quinces and cut them into cubes. Add the quinces to the syrup and let them cook for 10 to 15 minutes, until tender. Strain them and put them on kitchen paper to dry. Put them aside in a cool place. Keep the syrup.

Make a chocolate mousse by melting the chocolate with 200 g sugar in a *bain-marie* or double-boiler. Keep stirring until the chocolate has melted. Remove the pan from the heat and beat in the 6 egg yolks. In another bowl, beat the egg whites to stiff peaks and fold them into the chocolate mixture as soon as it has cooled.

Butter the charlotte tin. Dip the sponge fingers into the quince syrup one by one and cover the bottom and sides of the tin with them. You have to do this quickly, or they will fall apart in the syrup.

Spoon alternate layers of chocolate mousse and cooked quince into the tin, ending with a layer of mousse. Cover this with greaseproof paper or clingfilm. Put a plate on top and weigh it down lightly. Put the charlotte tin in the fridge overnight to set.

Turn out the charlotte onto a serving platter and decorate with grated chocolate.

The quince, coing, membrillo, marmelata, pyrus cydonia or portugalensis; emblem of love and happiness to the Ancients, was the golden fruit of the Hesperides, and the love-apple which Greek maidens gave their boys. It was also a symbol of long life and passion. I behold it in an emblem of the civilization of Europe, with its hard flesh, bright colour and unearthly savour. The simple flower, the astringent fruit which ripens only in the south, the mysterious pips full of emulgent oil – all are significant. There are artists like quinces, 'of quaint and loose habit,' their fragrance does not cloy.

Cyril Connolly ('Palinurus'), *The Unquiet Grave*, 1945

The realm of fig and quince: Spain and Portugal

Quince: *Membrillo* (Sp); *marmelo* (P)
Fig: *Higo* (Sp); *figo* (P)

What could be more fitting than a poem by a Spanish shepherd, who must have spent a lot of time under fig trees in the sweltering *campo* of Orihuela (Valencia) in his youth? The tree features prominently in the work of this poet, one of the casualties of the Spanish Civil War, who died at the age of thirty-nine.

> *Opened: sweet female genitals*
> *Green or black*
> *Tiny violet wine bags*
> *Closed: procreated like*
> *Dying hours and smooth*
>
> Miguel Hernández

In the course of centuries, little seems to have changed in the regional and traditional character of Spanish food. Occasionally a new dish appears, like the inspired *alioli de membrillo*, a quince-garlic relish from the Catalan Pyrenees, where the tree grows in the wild. In the past five decades tourism has had enormous consequences on the Spanish coasts, where menus of squid and bull's testicles have been replaced by photos of steaks and chips to accommodate the delicate stomachs of northern Europeans who make the trek to Spain with an arsenal of Rennies.

Simplicity and dignity: these are the words that I find best to characterize the land of Don Juan and Don Quixote, of the Alhambra and the Sagrada Família, of *tapas* and *paella*.

The fig tree's silhouette is never far away in the Iberian landscape. In Portugal, where the climate is Atlantic, the fig has also long been a main component of a meal. Portuguese cooking still shows the marks of Arabic influence; the Arabs introducing cane sugar, almonds, various fruits and the use of fresh herbs like mint, coriander and watercress.

The quince has an historic role in Portugal, if only because we derive our word 'marmalade' from the Portuguese word for quince, *marmelo*. It originally meant 'quince jam' and was made back in the Middle Ages, mainly in monasteries, with cane sugar from the Portuguese colonies like Madeira. Perhaps this is why Portuguese sweets often have ecclesiastical names, such as *jesuitas*, *papos de anjo* and *barrigas de freira* (Jesuits, angel biscuits and friars' bellies).

The first recipe from Spain is a remarkably flavourful aïoli made from quinces; it serves to enrich any meal, whether as an appetizer on the *meze* or *tapa* table, or with roast lamb or chicken, or as a dip for the prawns on page 92. It can be made by hand with a large pestle and mortar or in a food processor.

ALIOLI DE MEMBRILLO – QUINCE AÏOLI

To distinguish it from the common aïoli, I have baptized this sauce 'quaïoli'.

> *1 large quince*
> *3 or 4 cloves of garlic*
> *1 tsp sea salt*
> *75 ml fragrant olive oil*
> *juice of half a lemon*
> *1 tbsp honey, or to taste*

Peel and core the quince and chop it. Just cover with water and boil until soft.

Drain the quince pieces and put them in the bowl of a food processor with the salt. Add the garlic while the machine is running. Alternatively, crush the garlic with the salt in a mortar and add the quince pulp.

Pour in the olive oil in a thin stream while the machine is running, the same way as when you are making mayonnaise, until the oil is fully absorbed by the quince.

Stir in lemon juice and honey. Adjust the taste by adding salt and/or some more lemon juice. Let the 'quaïoli' cool in the fridge.

SALADA DE ESPINAFRE COM FIGOS E VINHO DO PORTO
SPINACH SALAD WITH FIGS AND PORT WINE

A variation on the spinach salad with pine nuts and raisins that you find everywhere on the Iberian Peninsula, as well as in other Mediterranean countries.

175 g dried figs
120 ml port
1 shallot, chopped
1 tsp sugar
1 ½ tsp chopped rosemary
30 g soft goat's cheese
25 g chopped pistachio nuts
2 tbsp balsamic vinegar
2 tsp Dijon mustard
salt, pepper
2 tbsp olive oil
450 g fresh spinach
half a red onion, thinly sliced

Cut the stems off the figs. Take 8 figs and cut a small cross in them on the stem side. Chop the rest.

Put the whole and the chopped figs in a saucepan with the port, shallot, sugar and rosemary. Cover and bring to a boil, then turn down the heat and simmer for 2 minutes. Remove the pan from the heat and let the figs cool for a quarter of an hour.

In the meantime, make little balls from the goat's

cheese – with moist hands or with two spoons – and roll them in chopped pistachio nuts. Keep in the fridge until just before serving time.

Add the balsamic vinegar, mustard, salt and pepper to the fig mixture in the pan. Stir in the olive oil. Put the dressing on low heat until warmed through.

Wash and dry the spinach and put it in a salad bowl. Put the red onion slices on top.

Remove the whole figs from the sauce and stuff them with cheese balls.

Pour the warm fig sauce over the spinach and divide the salad over four plates. Add the stuffed figs and serve immediately.

PIXIN A LA ASTURIANA
ASTURIAN MONKFISH WITH QUINCES

On the verdant northern coast of Spain, this sea monster, with its large head and the horns it uses to lure other fish, is prepared with a slightly sour sauce that combines very well with its flavour and slightly crustacean texture. This dish is usually eaten with potatoes fried in olive oil.

> *1 onion, chopped*
> *2 cloves of garlic, crushed*
> *1 ripe tomato, peeled and chopped*
> *2 quinces, peeled, cored and chopped*
> *1 tsp tomato purée*
> *250 ml cider or apple juice*
> *pinch of cayenne pepper*
> *salt, black pepper*
> *4 fillets from large monkfish tails*
> *1 tbsp lemon juice*
> *3 tbsp flour*
> *olive oil*

Sautée the onion in 2 tablespoons olive oil and add the garlic as soon as the onion has softened. Add tomato and quinces and sprinkle with a little cayenne. Stir in the cider or apple juice and tomato purée and let stew for 15 minutes, until the quince has become quite tender. Season with cayenne, salt and black pepper and purée the sauce with a handheld mixer or by pressing through a sieve.

Sprinkle the fish fillets with lemon juice and roll them in flour. Heat a few tablespoons of olive oil in a pan and fry the fish until it is golden brown and just done, about 5 to 10 minutes, depending on the thickness.

Serve on a dish with the warm sauce.

 TRUCHAS RELLENAS – TROUT STUFFED WITH FIGS

This recipe makes a change from the classic *trucha a la navarra* with *jamón serrano*, the Spanish version of *prosciutto*. The spiced fig and pine nut stuffing is refreshing and perfectly complements the delicate flavour of the trout.

> *4 dried figs*
> *2 tbsp olive oil*
> *160 g onion, chopped*
> *2 cloves garlic, chopped*
> *1 tsp ground coriander seed*
> *½ tsp ground cinnamon*
> *30 g fresh bread crumbs*
> *juice of a small lemon*
> *2 tbsp pine nuts*
> *salt, pepper*
> *4 whole trout, cleaned and gutted*
> *lemon wedges for garnish*

Soak the figs for a quarter of an hour in hot water. Drain and chop them, set them aside.

Heat the oil in a frying pan on a medium heat and fry the onion and garlic until light brown, about 5 minutes.

Add the chopped figs and ground spices. Remove the pan from the heat and let everything cool off.

Brown the pine nuts gently in a splash of olive oil in a separate pan. Stir the bread crumbs, pine nuts and lemon juice into the fig mixture. Season with salt and pepper.

Sprinkle salt and pepper in the cavity of the trout and spoon in the stuffing. Tie the trout up with thin cooking string. Put the stuffed fish in the fridge until about half an hour before serving. Preheat the oven to 200°C. Grease an oven dish lightly with olive oil and put the fish in side by side. Bake the fish for 15 to 20 minutes until done.

Remove the string and serve with lemon wedges.

CONEJO CON MEMBRILLO – RABBIT WITH QUINCE

I never ate so much rabbit as when I lived in Spain in the 1960s; they were cheap and truly wild and a good alternative to the local beef, which was of poor quality. Here are two recipes for rabbit: one with quince and one with figs. Use a good, full-bodied Rioja wine for the first dish; contrary to common assumption, the quality of the wine determines the quality of the dish.

The recipes for making *membrillo* are on pages 42–48, but you could always buy it ready-made from a delicatessen, which will also sell you the *jamón serrano* you need for the succeeding recipe.

1 large rabbit, or 2 small ones (the total weight should be
approximately 1 ½ kg), cut into pieces
120 g flour
120 ml olive oil
2 large onions, cut in half-moon wedges
12 garlic cloves (whole)
2 quinces, peeled, cored and cut into pieces
60 g dulce de membrillo, cubed
150 g tomato, peeled and chopped
3 cups Rioja wine
fresh parsley, chopped
salt, pepper

Mix the flour with salt and pepper and roll the rabbit pieces in it. Heat the olive oil in a thick-bottomed pan and brown the rabbit on all sides. Remove the pieces from the pan and set aside.

Put the onion, garlic cloves and quince in the pan and sautée them on low heat until soft, about 10 minutes. Add a dash of olive oil if necessary and scrape the bottom of the pan to release the tidbits stuck to it.

Now add the *membrillo*, tomatoes and wine. Bring to a boil, return the rabbit pieces to the pan, turn down the heat and let it simmer for one hour.

Season to taste and stir in the chopped parsley.

CONEJO CON HIGOS – RABBIT WITH FIGS

> *1 large rabbit or 2 small ones, cut into joints*
> *1 tsp dried thyme*
> *1 tsp dried sage*
> *olive oil for frying*
> *50 g* jamón serrano, *cut into strips*
> *150 g onion, chopped*
> *2 cloves garlic, chopped*
> *1 large carrot, chopped*
> *180 ml dry sherry*
> *180 ml chicken stock*
> *2 bay leaves*
> *8 fresh, firm figs, sliced in half*
> *salt and pepper*

Rub the salt, pepper, thyme and sage into the rabbit pieces.

Heat a few tablespoons of olive oil in a large frying pan and brown the rabbit on all sides. Remove the meat from the pan and set aside.

Fry the onion, carrot, garlic and ham for about 5 minutes, adding more olive oil if needed.

Douse with the sherry and stock and deglaze the pan. Return the rabbit to it and let it simmer on low heat for about 45 minutes. Add the figs and simmer for another 15 minutes.

FIGOS EN MADEIRA COM ARROZ DOCE
FIGS IN MADEIRA WITH RICE PUDDING

Madeira comes from the Portuguese island of the same name in the Atlantic and is of the same family of wines as port, which hails from Oporto: a powerful, amber-coloured dessert wine that lends itself very well to kitchen use, especially in puddings. Rice is cultivated in many places along the coast of Portugal.

for the figs
360 ml Madeira
1 tbsp clover or acacia honey
12 fresh figs, halved

for the rice pudding
1 lemon
1 orange
100 g pudding rice
pinch of salt
1 litre milk
1 cinnamon stick
100 g sugar
15 g butter
2 egg yolks
ground cinnamon

Bring the Madeira and the honey to a boil in a saucepan large enough to hold all the figs. Turn down the heat and let it simmer for 5 minutes.

Add the figs and poach them for 5 minutes. Let them cool in the wine.

To make the rice pudding, either grate or zest the orange and lemon peels (wash the fruit if not organic). Bring the rice to a boil in the milk with the peel, the cinnamon stick and a pinch of salt. Over a very low heat, let it simmer until the milk has been absorbed by the rice (about 20 minutes). Keep stirring regularly to avoid any sticking or burning. Take off the heat.

At this point, remove the cinnamon stick and add the sugar, the butter and the egg yolks. Allowing just enough heat to continue cooking, but not so much that it boils, keep stirring until the rice is very creamy, about 5 minutes. If it boils, the yolks will grain.

It is possible to make a rice pudding of this sort (boiled, not baked) in a double-boiler. It takes quite a lot longer, but you can be sure that the yolks will not be overheated.

Let the pudding cool in the fridge, sprinkle it with cinnamon and serve it with the figs in another bowl to one side.

MORGADA DE FIGOS – FIG SWEETS

What an invention, this treat, which is the fig's answer to *membrillo*. I have made it both with and without cocoa, with great success, and I have cut it into small squares or rolled it into little balls. I have also experimented with herbs: if you use fennel seeds instead of cinnamon, it is reminiscent of the Italian *salame di fichi*, which you slice like a sausage.

> *250 g blanched almonds*
> *250 g dried figs*
> *250 g sugar*
> *50 g cocoa powder*
> *½ tsp ground cinnamon*
> *grated peel of half a lemon*
> *caster or icing sugar*

Grind the almonds to a powder in a coffee grinder or food processor.

Remove the stems from the figs and soak the fruit in hot water for 10–15 minutes.

Put 100 ml water in a thick-bottomed pan with the sugar and bring to a boil. Keep stirring until the sugar has dissolved. Turn off the heat.

Remove the figs from their soaking water and chop them finely in a food processor. Put them in a bowl and mix in the almonds, cocoa, lemon peel and cinnamon.

Add this mixture to the syrup and let it thicken over a low heat, stirring continuously, until it has become a heavy mass that comes away from the sides of the pan.

Sprinkle some caster sugar on the bottom of a flat dish or baking sheet and spread the fig paste onto it in an even layer. Let it cool and harden, then cut it into squares or roll it into balls. Sprinkle with icing sugar or roll in cane sugar.

In honour of the Portuguese origins of marmalade, I close this chapter with several recipes for quince jam and jelly.

 *MARMELADA DE MARMELO* – QUINCE JAM (1)

> *750 g sugar*
> *1 litre water*
> *4 large quinces*

Put the water and the sugar in a large pan and bring to a boil. Stir until the sugar has dissolved.

Wash, peel and core the quinces. Tie the cores and peel in a piece of cheese-cloth and grate the quinces into the pan with the syrup. Stir well and add the bundle of peel and pips.

Let simmer on low heat until it becomes a transparent, orange-pink and rather thick mass. Remove the cheese-cloth bag and let simmer for another 5 minutes. Test the jam by letting a drop fall on a plate: it should congeal at once.

Put the jam in sterilized jars and turn them upside down for 5 minutes.

❧ *MARMELADA DE MARMELO* – QUINCE JAM (2)

quinces
750 g sugar to 1 kg of quince pulp or
600 g honey to 1 kg of quince pulp

Wash the quinces and quarter them. Put them in a large pan, just cover them with water and let them cook over medium heat for about a half hour. Remove the quinces from the pan with a slotted spoon and let them cool.

Once cool, peel and core them. Chop them finely or purée them. Add this pulp back to the cooking liquid and weigh the result. Add 750 g sugar or 600 g honey to each kilogram of quince pulp.

Bring to the boil and cook the mixture, stirring, for another 45 minutes, or until set.

Put in sterilized jam jars and close tightly.

❧ *MARMELADA DE MARMELO* – QUINCE JAM (3)

Having made either the first or the second recipe, add lemon juice, ground cinnamon, cloves, ginger or cardamom before putting it into jars. In some countries they add lemon leaves or apple geranium (*Pelargonium odoratissimum*) to flavour the jam.

ع‏ *MARMELADA DE MARMELO* – QUINCE JAM (4)

If the quince harvest is meagre, you can add apples to make this delicious 'quapple' jam.

> *1 kg quinces*
> *500 g apples*
> *2 tbsp lemon juice*
> *at least 1 kg sugar*

Wash the quinces and apples and cut them in pieces or slices. Put the fruit just under water in a thick-bottomed pan. Let simmer on low heat until done.

Strain the fruit, saving the liquid, which you can use to make a separate jelly.

Purée the fruit and weigh it. Add the same weight in sugar. Stir in the lemon juice and let everything boil down before putting it in sterilized jars.

ع‏ *MARMELADA DE MARMELO* – QUINCE JELLY

Quince jelly is made from the cooking liquid in which unpeeled and uncored quinces have been boiled. Make a jelly with nearly the same amount of sugar (or use preserving sugar and follow the instructions on the packet).

The realm of fig and quince: the Maghreb – Morocco, Tunisia and Algeria

Quince: *Sfergel, Coing*
Fig: *Lkrmos, Figue*

It is yellow in colour, as if it wore a daffodil
Tunic, and it smells like musk, a penetrating smell.

It has the perfume of a loved woman and the same
Hardness of heart, but it has the colour of the
Impassioned and scrawny lover.

Its pallor is borrowed from my pallor; its smell
Is my sweetheart's breath.

When it stood fragrant on the bough and the leaves
Had woven for it a covering of brocade,

I gently put up my hand to pluck it and to set it
Like a censer in the middle of my room.

It had a cloak of ash-coloured down hovering over
Its smooth golden body,

And when it lay naked in my hand, with nothing
More than
Its daffodil-coloured shift,

> *It made me think of her I cannot mention, and I feared*
> *The ardour of my breath would shrivel it in my fingers.*
>
> *Isn't that Aphrodite's apple?*

This sensual riddle in verse was composed in the tenth century by the Moorish-Andalusian poet and vizier Shafer ben Utman al-Mushafi.

Tajine, harissa, couscous, ras el hanout: these are a few key words that gain us access to the Maghreb kitchen. Maghreb, the Arabic word for the West, is the region between the peaks of the Atlas mountains and the Mediterranean, the countries of Morocco, Tunisia and Algeria. The words and their meaning will be elucidated in the recipes that follow. In the cuisine of the Maghreb we find the influences of the Sephardic Jews who settled there, of the Berbers, who had expanded their empire to Spain in the twelfth century, and of the Middle Eastern caliphate, especially Baghdad. Later, the influence of the French was of course added to this.

A characteristic feature of Maghreb cooking is the way it combines meat (*ghalmi*, lamb and mutton, in particular) with fresh vegetables and fruit and spices in *tajines* – a kind of stew that is both tasty and healthy and offers many possibilities for the fruits that concern us in this book, the quince and the fig. Preserved lemons are often added for zest, and for those who do not have access to a Middle Eastern market, I offer a recipe for preserved lemons ready to use within five days, as well as one for *harissa*, the Tunisian answer to the south-east Asian sambal.

The exclusively Moroccan argan oil has quickly become the latest culinary fad. This remarkably flavoured oil is made from the stones of the argan fruit; the tree (*Argana spinosa*) is native to the south-western part of Morocco, mainly around Essaouira. The tree is famous for its attractiveness to goats, which climb up to the very top, making a bizarre and comic spectacle. The oil is quite delicious and has a nutty, fruity and powerful flavour, very good on a salad of oranges and olives, but it is not really suited for frying. Argan oil is imported on a small scale and sold at an absurdly high price, chiefly because of its labour-intensive production. The same can of course be said of some olive oils.

As far as herbs and spices are concerned we can have recourse to *ras el hanout* ('top of the shop'), which is a ready-made mixture of ten or twenty or more spices – in some regions they have even been known to add the aphrodisiac Spanish fly (cantharides, now a forbidden item) – or we can put together a different combination of spices for every dish. North African cooking nearly always contains cumin, coriander, cardamom, cinnamon (the four Cs) and turmeric. These are balanced by the various peppers: white, black, cayenne and chilli.

After the meal – or over a water pipe, with or without the addition of opium – the *barrad* appears: a gleaming silver teapot with a bell-shaped lid, from which the green tea with fresh mint is poured out in a high arc, to spread the aroma and intoxicate us with the fragrance.

❧ *L'HAMED MREQUED* – PRESERVED LEMONS

Lemons preserved in this way do not keep for very long but are intended for consumption after a mere five days in their brine, in the absence of fruit that has been prepared for longer storage.

> *lemons*
> *salt*
> *water*
> *coriander seeds and cinnamon sticks (optional)*

Score the peel of the lemons from top to bottom 4 or 6 times (do not cut too deep, or the juice will run out).

Rub some salt into the lemons and put them in a saucepan with salty water and, to taste, a teaspoon of coriander seeds and a small stick of cinnamon.

Boil the lemons until the skin is quite soft. Put the lemons in a large preserving jar and top up with the cooking liquid. If the liquid doesn't cover them, add some fresh lemon juice. Ready for use after five days.

HARISSA – TUNISIAN CHILLI SAUCE

Harissa can be made at home with a pestle and mortar or in a food processor. It will keep for several weeks in the fridge.

> *60 g dried red chillies*
> *3 fresh red chillies*
> *4 garlic cloves*
> *2 tbsp cumin seed*
> *1 tbsp coriander seed*
> *½ tsp salt*
> *olive oil*

Soak the dried chillies in hot water for half an hour to an hour. Toast the cumin and coriander seeds in a dry pan for 2 to 3 minutes. Keep them moving around the pan and try not to burn them.

If you are making this by hand, put the toasted seeds in the mortar, add the peeled garlic and the salt and pound everything to a fine paste. Alternatively, grind the seeds finely in a coffee or spice grinder and add these to the garlic which you have pounded in the mortar with the salt.

Add all the chillies to the mortar and continue pounding to make a paste. Add some olive oil little by little until the paste is thick and smooth.

Put the *harissa* in a clean, dry jar, cover with a layer of olive oil and screw on the lid. Keep in the fridge.

As variations, you can add half a bunch of fresh coriander leaves, chopped, at the end; or you can use caraway seeds instead of cumin.

PAIN DE FIGUES — FIG BREAD

> *He thought it well, as he did, to make voyage to a place*
> *called Shershel, twenty leagues from Algiers on the Oran*
> *side, where there is an extensive trade in dried figs.*
> Cervantes, *Don Quixote*

Khobz, bread, an indispensable part of Maghreb food, is offered at each and every meal. Turkish and Moroccan flatbreads have become common in Western Europe. The lightly sweetened fig bread described here is a fitting complement to a generous and varied *meze* table or to one of the *tajines* that follow.

> *1 sachet (7 g) instant dried yeast*
> *1 tsp sugar*
> *1 tsp salt*
> *grated peel of 1 orange*
> *approximately 225 g strong bread flour*
> *240 ml lukewarm water*
> *2 tbsp olive oil*
> *175 g dried figs*
> *180 ml water*
> *½ tsp ground allspice*

Combine all the dry ingredients in a bowl. Make a well in the middle and add most of the lukewarm water and the olive oil. Stir this into the dry ingredients with your hands and bring it to a homogenous mass. Add the final drops of water, unless the dough is very slack and sticky. Once a tidy ball, bring the dough onto a floured work-surface and knead it for 5 minutes.

Put the dough in an oiled bowl, cover with a clean tea towel and let it rise in a warm place until doubled in size, usually about one hour.

In the meantime, put the figs in 180 ml water with the allspice. Boil them until they form a thick, soft pulp. Purée the figs in a blender. Let them cool.

Punch the risen dough and knead the air bubbles out of it. On a floured worktop or board, roll it out to a rectangle that is approximately the same size as your baking sheet. Spread the fig purée on the dough and roll it up as if it were a Swiss roll. Fold the ends under. Place the loaf on an oiled baking sheet and brush with a little olive oil. Let it rest in a warm place, covered with a moist tea towel, for about half an hour. Preheat the oven to 180–200°C.

Bake the bread for half an hour until it is light brown.

TAJINES

A *tajine* is a stew, named for the earthenware dish with a pointed lid in which it is cooked and served. These dishes can be used in the oven, like Spanish earthenware (which could be used instead), or on top of a gas cooker. Of course you could make a *tajine* in an ordinary pan, but the result will be less fragrant and tender. A *tajine* is usually served with bread and/or couscous, fresh herbs and *harissa*.

TAJINE MAA LKRMOS – FIG *TAJINE*

> *2 onions, chopped*
> *2 garlic cloves, chopped*
> *2 tbsp olive oil*
> *2 cinnamon sticks*
> *2 tsp* ras el hanout
> *2 red onions, sliced*
> *500 ml vegetable stock*
> *500 g pumpkin flesh, chopped*
> *8 dried figs*
> *4 large fresh figs, halved*
> *100 g shelled pistachio nuts*
> *½ bunch fresh mint*
> *salt, pepper*

Heat the oil on medium heat in a *tajine* or pan and fry the onion and garlic until they are transparent. Add the cinnamon sticks and *ras el hanout*.

Cover this with a layer of the sliced red onions and pour in the vegetable stock, which you should heat before adding. Add the pumpkin and figs, salt and pepper to taste and let it all stew gently for half an hour.

Garnish with pistachio nuts and mint leaves just before serving.

 *LHOT MAA SFERGEL – FISH WITH QUINCES*

This is a recipe by the British-Egyptian food writer and historian Claudia Roden, the uncrowned queen of Middle Eastern cooking. She says she got the idea for this dish by combining two Moroccan recipes.

> *3 tbsp vegetable oil*
> *4 garlic cloves, chopped finely*
> *500 g tomatoes, peeled and chopped*
> *1 tsp sugar*
> *pinch salt*
> *1 chilli, halved, with seeds removed*
> *1 piece of fresh ginger, approx. 1 centimetre, peeled*
> *2 quinces*
> *800 g fish fillets (a firm fish like cod or haddock)*
> *green coriander*

Heat the oil in a large frying pan and fry the garlic until it starts to colour. Add the tomatoes, sugar, salt and chilli and turn the heat down. Squeeze the juice from the ginger into the pan with a garlic crusher.

Peel and core the quinces, slice them and put them immediately into the sauce to prevent them from discolouring. Let the sauce simmer for half an hour, uncovered, until the quince is cooked. When you think the sauce is spicy enough, remove the chilli.

Around ten minutes before serving, put the fish fillets in the sauce and let them simmer till done. Serve with couscous and garnish with coriander.

DEGAG MAA QUQULA
CHICKEN WITH QUINCE AND CARDAMOM

This French-Algerian recipe calls for three of the four spices beginning with the letter C I talked of earlier. I envy those who have yet to discover the incredibly subtle flavour of cardamom: your life will never be quite the same! The recipe will serve 6 people.

> *1 large chicken or 2 small ones, cut into pieces, skin removed*
> *3 limes: the grated zest of 1 lime, the juice of 2 limes and some slices of lime for the finish*
> *1 piece of ginger root (a two-centimetre cube)*
> *250 ml plain yoghurt*
> *10 cardamom pods*
> *2 cloves garlic, finely chopped*
> *½ tsp cumin seeds*
> *1 tbsp turmeric*
> *pinch of cayenne pepper*
> *butter*
> *2 onions, chopped*
> *1 big or 2 small quinces*
> *½ bunch green coriander*

Put the chicken pieces side by side in a shallow dish, season with salt and pepper and squeeze the juice of two limes over the meat (after you have grated the zest of one of them).

Grate the ginger into the yoghurt, remove the black seeds from the cardamom pods and add them to the yoghurt with the garlic, the cumin, turmeric, cayenne and the grated lime zest. Mix well and spread over the chicken pieces. Let it marinate in the fridge for at least three hours, turning the pieces once or twice.

Melt the butter in a large casserole and sautée the onions until transparent. Remove the core from the quinces (no need to peel them) and slice them thinly. Fry them briefly with the onions. Remove onions and quince from the pan with a slotted spoon and set them aside.

Remove the chicken from the marinade, reserving the marinade, and fry them in a little more butter in the same casserole until they are browned all over.

Add a glass of water (or stock) and return the onion and quince to the pan, along with the marinade. Simmer the chicken on low heat with the lid half-covering the pan for about half an hour, until just done.

Garnish the chicken before serving with small slices of lime and chopped coriander.

CHEVREAU MI-FIGUE, MI-RAISIN
ROAST KID WITH FIGS AND GRAPES

A French-Tunisian recipe that does full justice to the slightly sweetish flavour of the kid, which is looked on askance by some and considered inferior to lamb. It can be found at Islamic butchers and requires the same preparation as lamb. Count on a cooking time of 20 minutes per pound (500 g), a little longer for boneless meat; meat with bones (the bones conduct the heat) and meat that has been frozen is done more quickly.

> *1 leg or shoulder of kid*
> *olive oil*
> *juice of 1 lemon*
> *½ tsp each of ground cumin, coriander and turmeric*
> *8 fresh figs*
> *250 g grapes, green and black mixed*
> *40 g whole blanched almonds*
> *150 ml Banyuls (a dessert wine from the south of*
> *France), port or Madeira*
> *salt, pepper*

Preheat the oven to 200°C. Put the meat in an oiled oven dish and rub it all over with the spices, olive oil and lemon juice. Put the dish in the oven and roast for 10 minutes, then turn the heat down to 180°C.

Prepare the fruit while the meat is roasting. Wash the figs and make incisions in them with a sharp knife (from top to bottom). Wash the grapes and remove the seeds if you desire. Arrange the fruit around the meat a quarter of an hour before the end of cooking time and scatter the almonds all over. Pour in the wine and leave the dish in the oven until the meat is done. Let it rest for 10 or 15 minutes before serving.

A tajine sitting on a pottery charcoal brazier.

TAJINE GHALMI MAA SFERGEL
TAJINE OF LAMB AND QUINCES

Lamb *tajines* can be found across the entire Maghreb region in innumerable variants, depending on the season and the fruit or vegetables available. I am offering three recipes here: one just with quince, one with quince and figs (which began as a *tajine* with quince and prunes) and one with quince and okra. In each case, don't forget to put the *harissa* on the table.

> *1 to 1.5 kg boneless lamb, shoulder or leg, cut into cubes*
> *salt to taste*
> *pinch of turmeric*
> *1 tsp ground ginger*
> *1 tsp freshly ground black pepper*
> *¼ tsp cayenne pepper*
> *50 g grated onion*
> *45 g butter*
> *2 tbsp chopped parsley*
> *40 g chopped onion*
> *500 g quince*
> *lemon juice*
> *1 cinnamon stick*
> *honey, ground cinnamon*

Remove as much visible fat from the meat as possible. Mix the salt, spices, grated onion, butter and parsley in the *tajine*, let them fry lightly for a few minutes to release the aromas, then add the meat. Stir, but do not brown.

Add two cups of water, bring to a boil and simmer for an hour on low heat with the lid on.

Add the chopped onion and simmer for another 45 minutes, until the meat is done and the sauce has thickened somewhat.

Wash the quinces and core them. Boil them in water with lemon juice and the cinnamon stick till just tender. Do not let them fall apart. Remove the quince from the water with a slotted spoon and set aside.

Halve the quinces and arrange them on top of the meat about 15 minutes before serving time. Drizzle a spoonful of honey over the whole and dust with some ground cinnamon.

TAJINE OF LAMB SHANK WITH QUINCE AND DRIED FIGS (OR PRUNES)

The shank is the tenderest part of the leg; when stewed slowly, the meat falls off the bones in succulent morsels. Have the butcher saw through the bone, so that the marrow may add to the flavour.

> *1 lamb shank per person*
> *1 large onion, chopped*
> *30 g butter*
> *salt, pepper*
> *½ tsp ground cinnamon*
> *½ tsp turmeric*
> *½ tsp allspice*
> *1 tbsp tomato paste*
> *360 ml water*
> *10 dried figs*
> *1 quince*
> *fresh coriander leaves for garnishing*

Heat the butter in the *tajine* and sweat the onion on low heat until golden. Put the meat in the pan and sprinkle over the salt and spices. Add the tomato paste and the water and stir well. Add the figs, with their little hard stems removed. Let everything simmer very slowly for an hour to an hour and a half.

Add the quince, cored and quartered. Stew for about another hour – the meat should be virtually falling off the bone. Serve with sprigs of coriander and couscous.

TAJINE OF LAMB WITH QUINCE AND OKRA

Okra is an intriguing vegetable which should be prepared with care or it will become slimy. It should be left whole and not stirred too vigorously. In North Africa the vegetable is usually soaked in olive oil and salt first. This recipe should serve six people.

> *500 g fresh okra*
> *1 tbsp salt, mixed with a little black pepper*
> *olive oil*
> *3 quinces*
> *lemon juice*
> *1 chopped red onion*
> *½ tsp turmeric*
> *1-cm piece of fresh ginger root, grated*
> *1 tsp ground cumin*
> *½ tsp ground coriander seeds*
> *1 cinnamon stick*
> *2 very small dried red chillies, seeds removed*
> *cloves from half a head of garlic, peeled*
> *1 kg boneless lamb, cut into cubes*
> *120 ml (lamb) stock made from the bones you have removed*
> *fresh coriander*

Cut the stems from the okra, but be careful not to cut open the ladies' fingers themselves. Put them in a bowl with a little olive oil and the salt/pepper mixture for half an hour.

Wash the quinces, core them and cut each of them into six segments. Put them in water with some lemon juice to prevent browning.

Put the onion with 3 tablespoons of olive oil, the turmeric, ginger, cumin, coriander, the cinnamon stick, chillies and the peeled garlic in a *tajine* on medium heat. Add the lamb and stir to coat and brown lightly. Add the stock and 1 cup of water and let everything simmer for about one hour. Add a little more water or stock if it gets too dry.

Parboil the quinces for 10 minutes and arrange them on the meat in the *tajine*. Let everything simmer for another half hour and serve garnished with fresh coriander.

Now we come to the desserts, which in North Africa are extremely sweet – just think of baklava and Turkish delight! There appears to be a law of nature that says the hotter the climate, the sweeter the puddings. In a (sub) tropical country, people may need the extra boost that is provided by the sugar (or honey).

PURÉE DE COINGS AUX ABRICOTS ET AMANDES
QUINCE PURÉE WITH APRICOTS AND ALMONDS

> *2 large quinces (total weight approx. 500 g)*
> *8 dried apricots*
> *4 tbsp ground almonds*
> *100 g sugar*
> *½ tsp ground cinnamon*
> *½ tsp ground ginger*
> *freshly grated nutmeg*

Peel and core quinces, quarter them and put them with the apricots in a pan. Barely cover them with water. Bring to the boil, turn down the heat and let them simmer until the fruit is very soft and has taken on a lovely orange colour. Remove the fruit with a slotted spoon, but reserve the liquid.

Grind the almonds, add the quinces and apricots and a cup of the liquid to make a thin purée.

Put the purée in a saucepan with the sugar and spices and cook it for 10 minutes, stirring, until the mixture has thickened.

Spoon the purée into a serving bowl and let it cool. Sprinkle with nutmeg and caster sugar before serving.

TARTE DE FIGUES AUX NOIX – FIG TART WITH WALNUTS

This dish makes a good finish for a (not too heavy) meal, with or without whipped cream flavoured with a few drops of orange-flower water.

for the dough
240 g plain flour
1 tbsp sugar
pinch of salt
120 g butter, cubed
1 to 3 tbsp water

for the filling
125 g walnuts
60 g caster sugar
2 tbsp plain flour
25 g butter
1 egg
1 tbsp brandy
1 tbsp grated orange peel
9 fresh figs

Mix the dough in a food processor as follows: put the flour, sugar and salt in the bowl of the machine and pulse a few times to mix it well. Add the butter cubes and blend until the mixture is coarsely grained. Pour a little water into the machine while it is running, until the dough comes away from the sides. Roll the dough into a ball, flatten it and wrap it in plastic. Put it in the fridge for half an hour.

Prepare the filling: toast the walnuts in a dry frying pan for 2 minutes and let them cool. Grind the nuts finely in the processor with half the caster sugar. Sift the rest of the flour and sugar into the bowl and mix well. Add the butter, egg, brandy and orange peel and blend thoroughly. Put the mixture in a bowl.

Chop four of the figs into small pieces and add to the mixture in the bowl. Stir well.

Preheat the oven to 200°C. Roll out the dough and line a greased tart ring with it. Bake blind in the oven for 15 minutes (line the dough with baking parchment filled with dried beans).

Cut the rest of the figs in thin slices. Remove the pastry from the oven, discard the beans and paper and pour in the fig mixture. Cover with slices of fig. Turn down the oven to 180°C. Return the tart to the oven and bake it for about 35 to 40 minutes until the filling is set and golden brown.

Bibliography

Antiphilos, from: *Eat, Drink and Be Merry*, ed. Peter Washington, Alfred A. Knopf, 2003.

Artusi, Pellegrino, *Science in the Kitchen and the Art of Eating Well*, University of Toronto Press, 2003.

Bellingham, David, *An Introduction to Greek Mythology*, Quintet Publishing Limited, London, 1989.

Braudel, Fernand, *Les Mémoires de la Mediterranée*, Ed. De Fallois, 1998.

Castlereagh, Duncan, *The Great Age of Exploration*, Aldus Books, 1971.

Cervantes de Saavedra, Miguel de, *Don Quixote de la Mancha*, London 1885.

Coleridge, Samuel, *Biographia Literaria*, Princeton University Press, 1984.

Cyril Connolly ('Palinurus'), *The Unquiet Grave*, Viking, 1945.

Culpeper, Nicholas, *The Complete Herbal*, W. Foulsham & Company Limited, London, 1983.

Dalby, Andrew and Sally Grainger, *The Classical Cookbook*, British Museum Press, 1996.

Dante, *Divine Comedy*.

David, Elizabeth, *Mediterranean Food*, Penguin, 1977.

Davidson, Alan, *The Penguin Companion to Food*, Penguin, 2002.

Degaudenzi, Jean-Louis, *Les Recettes de Nostradamus*, Ed. Joëlle Losfeld, 1999.

Dodoens, Rembertus, *Cruyd-Boeck (1554)*, L.J. Veen's Uitgeversmaatschappij N.V., Amsterdam.

Epictetus, from: *Eat, Drink and Be Merry*, ed. Peter Washington, Alfred A. Knopf, 2003.

Graves, Robert, *The Greek Myths*, Penguin, 1964.

Grigson, Jane, *Jane Grigson's Fruit Book*, Penguin, 1983.

Hadfield, Miles and John, *Gardens of Delight*, Cassell, 1964.

Hernández, Miguel, *Obra Completa*, Espasa-Calpe, 1993.

Khayyám, Omar, *Rubáiyát*, Dover Books, 1990.

Lawrence, D.H., *The Complete Poems*, Penguin, 1974.

Lear, Edward, *The Complete Nonsense of Edward Lear*, Faber & Faber, 1947.

Palter, Robert, *The Duchess of Malfi's Apricots and Other Literary Fruits*, University of South Carolina Press, 2002.

Pliny the Elder, *Naturalis Historia, De Wereld*, Uitgeverij Athenaeum-Polak & Van Gennep, Amsterdam, 2004.

Shafer ben Utman Al-Mushafi, from: *Eat, Drink and Be Merry*, ed. Peter Washington, Alfred A. Knopf, 2003.

Roden, Claudia, *The Book of Jewish Food*, Viking, 1996.

——, *Invitation to Mediterranean Cooking*, Rizzoli, 1997.

Theocritus, *The Idylls*, Penguin Classics, 1989.

Varone, Antonio and Erich Lessing, *Pompeii*, ed. Pierre Terrail, 1995.

Index of recipes